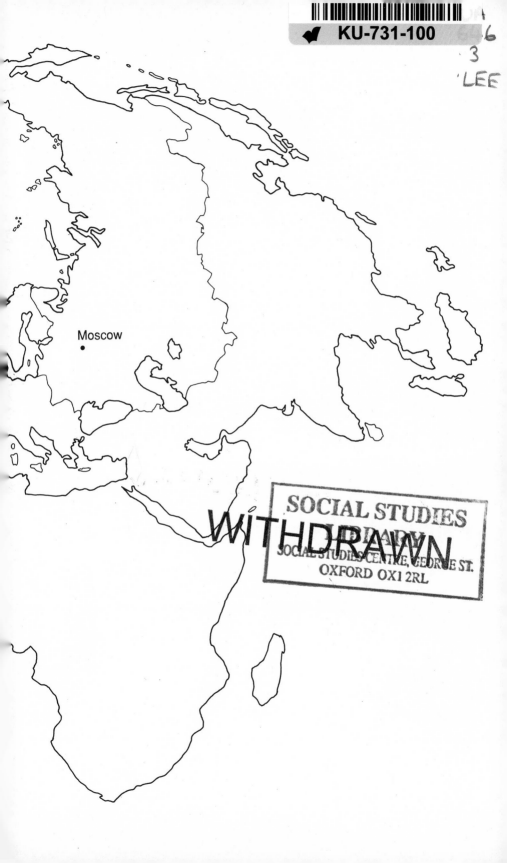

Moscow
•

Halt! Who Goes Where?

The Future of NATO in the New Europe

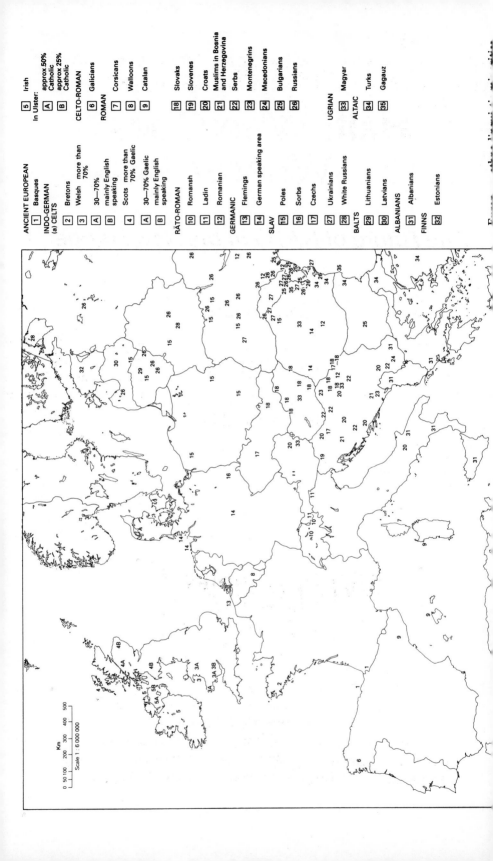

ANCIENT EUROPEAN

1 Basques

INDO-GERMAN
(a) CELTS

2 Bretons

3 Welsh more than 70%

A 30–70%

B mainly English speaking

4 Scots more than 70% Gaelic

A 30–70% Gaelic

B mainly English speaking

5 Irish
In Ulster:
A approx.50% Catholic
B approx 25% Catholic

CELTO-ROMAN

6 Galicians

ROMAN

7 Corsicans

8 Walloons

9 Catalan

RÄTO-ROMAN

10 Romansh

11 Ladin

12 Romanian

GERMANIC

13 Flemings

14 German speaking area

SLAV

15 Poles

16 Sorbs

17 Czechs

18 Slovaks

19 Slovenes

20 Croats

21 Muslims in Bosnia and Herzegovina

22 Serbs

23 Montenegrins

24 Macedonians

25 Bulgarians

26 Russians

27 Ukrainians

28 White Russians

BALTS

29 Lithuanians

30 Latvians

ALBANIANS

31 Albanians

FINNS

32 Estonians

UGRIAN

33 Magyar

ALTAIC

34 Turks

35 Gagauz

Halt! Who Goes Where?

The Future of NATO in the New Europe

by

JOHN LEECH

Foreword by
Frank C Carlucci

Introduction by
Michael Heseltine

BRASSEY'S (UK)

(Member of the Maxwell Macmillan Pergamon Publishing Corporation)

LONDON · OXFORD · WASHINGTON · NEW YORK · BEIJING
FRANKFURT · SÃO PAULO · SYDNEY · TOKYO · TORONTO

First English edition 1991

UK editorial offices: Brassey's, 50 Fetter Lane, London EC4A 1AA
orders: Brassey's, Headington Hill Hall, Oxford OX3 0BW

USA editorial offices: Brassey's, 8000 Westpark Drive, Fourth Floor, McLean, Virginia 22102
orders: Macmillan, Front and Brown Streets, Riverside, New Jersey 08075, USA

Distributed in North America to booksellers and wholesalers by the Macmillan Publishing Company, N.Y., N.Y.

Library of Congress Cataloging in Publication Data
Leech, John, 1925–
Halt! Who goes where?: the future of NATO in the new Europe/
John Leech; foreword by Frank Carlucci; introduction by Michael Heseltine—
1st English ed.
p. cm.
Includes index.
1. North Atlantic Treaty Organization. 2. Europe—National security. 3. Europe—
Military policy. 4. Europe—Politics and government—1945–   I. Title.
UA646.3.L345   1991   355'.031'091821—dc20   90–23338

British Library Cataloguing in Publication Data
Leech, John
Halt! Who goes where? : the future of NATO in the New Europe.
1. North Atlantic Treaty Organization
I Title
355.031091821

ISBN 0–08–040978–4

Printed in Great Britain by B.P.C.C. Wheatons Ltd, Exeter

Contents

Preface

THIS BOOK is based on ideas expressed at a meeting of some 40 eminent diplomats, academics, defence specialists, politicians and leaders in public affairs. Presided over by two former Ministers of Defence, Rt Hon Michael Heseltine MP and Hon Frank C Carlucci, they were drawn from the United States and five major European countries, including the German Democratic Republic.

A list of those who took part is included. The author has tried to draw together and develop the main strands of the discussion, but without individual attribution. The book is therefore not an agreed summary of proceedings, and not all the participants would necessarily wish to be identified with any particular view or statement.

The meeting was organised by WEST-WEST AGENDA, in association with the American Academy of Diplomacy. WEST-WEST AGENDA is a small Euro-American circle which concerns itself with the functioning of consultation and cohesion within the Atlantic partnership. Whilst its activities are normally conducted between individuals, it decided that the subject of 'The Future of NATO in the New Europe' could benefit from its ability to bring together a wider diversity of pertinent opinion on a theme which is normally reserved for the specialist.

Glossary

AMF	Allied Command Europe Mobile Force
ASEAN	Association of South-East Asian Nations
BAOR	British Army of the Rhine
CFE	Conventional Armed Forces in Europe Treaty
CIA	US Central Intelligence Agency
COMECON	Council for Mutual Economic Assistance
CSBMs	Conference on Security Building Measures
CSCE	Conference on Security and Co-operation in Europe
EBRD	European Bank for Reconstruction and Development
EC	European Community
ECOWAS	Economic Community of West African States
EFTA	European Free Trade Area
EP	European Parliament
FPP	NATO Force Planning Process
GATT	General Agreement on Tariffs and Trade
G-7	Group of Seven major industrial countries holding periodic economic co-ordination summits
IAEA	International Atomic Energy Agency
IBRD	International Bank for Reconstruction and Development (World Bank)
IEPG	Independent European Programme Group
IMF	International Monetary Fund
INF	Intermediate Nuclear Force (reductions)
NACISA	North Atlantic Communications and Information Systems Agency
NAMSCO	North Atlantic Maintenance and Supply Agency

NATO	North Atlantic Treaty Organisation
OECD	Organisation for Economic Co-operation and Development
SADCC	Southern Africa Development Co-ordination Conference
START	Strategic Arms Reduction Treaty
TASMs	Tactical air-to-surface missiles
UN	United Nations
WEU	Western European Union

Foreword

by

Hon Frank C Carlucci

I CAN recall, as a new Secretary of Defense, in late 1987 attending my first NATO Ministerial Meeting and coming away with my head swimming. How could so many spirited opinions and divergent points of view ever produce a coherent policy? Who was in charge here? I listened and I tried to learn. To this day I don't fully understand the process but, in my farewell comments to my colleagues, I referred to the NATO magic that somehow pulled it all together just in time to avert crisis and move policy forward. Oratorical excursions notwithstanding, it works.

And well. We have seen our most cherished dreams for Eastern Europe realised, and communism as a political force is spent. Yet we have been reminded by events in the Middle East that we do not live in a threat free world. Wherever there is instability—and there is much of that in the USSR and Eastern Europe—there are risks that even the most sophisticated cannot foresee.

Our job is to manage these risks while seizing the greatest opportunity of our generation. Several points seem clear. One is that the US must remain engaged. We must reject the counsel of the pessimists, the isolationists and the protectionists, even if the latter wrap themselves in the mantle of national security. US leadership is critical to world order. But to be effective that leadership must be exercised in collaboration with our allies, who are growing every day in strength and confidence. Our post-war policies have been a success, a development we should welcome. After all, the solidarity of the Atlantic Alliance is the best assurance for peace in Europe as well as for the management of common problems around an increasingly volatile globe. It is also the best assurance for the security of the United States.

A continued US military presence in Europe, even a reduced one, is an integral component of this strategy. Of course, NATO must change, as must the role of the United States in NATO. But these are the manageable issues born of success. NATO as an institution can and should endure for it is, in the words of its Secretary General, both an agent for change and an anchor. It is also the key to the preservation of the Atlantic Alliance.

John Leech poses all the right questions as NATO seeks its new role. Nobody has all the right answers at this point, but the kind of thoughtful analysis John provides will stimulate our thinking as we try to shape a new and stable balance of power in Central Europe.

Introduction

by

Rt Hon Michael Heseltine MP

'NATO IN CRISIS' has been a headline for over-enthusiastic sub-editors ever since its birth in 1949. In terms of the only thing that matters— the united resolve of NATO members to act together in the individual defence of any one member and in the collective defence of them all— such headlines have been grossly misleading. They merely reflect the truism that NATO is an alliance of parliamentary democracies, which thrive on open debate. The military reality has always been very different and much more reassuring.

For the first time since its foundation NATO genuinely has options. The choices are real.

My purpose here is to look at NATO in a European context. But, as an aside, the very arguments which we perceive as essentially based upon Europe and the NATO alliance have their mirror-image in the Pacific. If Soviet imperialism has been stood down, a changed perception of threat will have consequences for the democracies of the Pacific, potentially more difficult to handle even than those we face in Europe. The principal players are the same. The confrontation between political and economic pluralism and Soviet communism has engulfed the Pacific as comprehensively as it has Europe. If we now have to peer into the vacuum left by the reduction in tension between the superpowers, be very sure that there will be forces at work, seeking to muscle into that vacuum—not just here in Europe, but there in the Pacific as well. The attitude of Japan, in this context, will be crucial.

Some would argue: 'Now there is no threat, why an alliance?' But is it realistic to regard the Soviet threat as a thing of the past? If a threat consists of capability and intention then the question answers itself.

Soviet capability is, if anything, greater now than at any previous time. She has continued to modernise her weapons systems and any reductions have been of virtually redundant capability. I do not believe Mr Gorbachev has any intention of embarking upon an assault on western Europe, and any successor would face formidable difficulties in forcing Soviet troops across central European nations which have drawn the first breath of freedom and would fiercely object to such passage. But Soviet military might is still formidable and a residual threat certainly remains.

Nor are there grounds for basing our policy upon assumptions of stability in eastern Europe. The West will soon be deeply involved economically in central Europe and will pursue every means of promoting stability in the region. But Soviet withdrawal has opened up the opportunity for the re-emergence of historic rivalries. Economic reform will be neither smooth nor speedy. The crisis in the Gulf has already raised the costs, public expectations are bound to be disappointed and those hungry for power will readily exploit any passion to hand. An appeal to ethnic loyalty or national instinct is a potent weapon. Even if the original threat that led to NATO's formation has gone, the price of peace remains eternal vigilance and central Europe will be a potential trouble spot for some time to come.

Realistically, while we welcome the growing détente between the superpowers, managing that détente will require a greater degree of sophistication than the rather more focused threat of the past. It is here that NATO faces its next challenge. There are underway a range of negotiations affecting all classes of weapons systems. Certain objectives will, I believe, be common to all. We want to maintain stability and security. We want to do that at lower cost and, therefore, with fewer weapons and men. That requires complex and cautious negotiation. Success will depend upon continual monitoring and verification and will involve personnel moving back and forth through what was once the impenetrable Iron Curtain. The more coherent the western response, the more likely the process is to be successful.

On one side of the equation only the forces of the Soviet Union are now significant. They remain devastatingly destructive and highly professional. The picture on our side is more complicated. It involves the military capabilities of a united Germany, the independent nuclear deterrents of France and the UK and the US forces in Europe. If the Atlantic dimension is to remain credible, the maintenance of the NATO alliance is essential to preserve that coupling and to manage the process of peace. The most persuasive argument against any new arms build-up or confrontation, whoever the protagonist, is the knowledge that the West remains strong and united.

That requires three conditions: first, the achievement of verifiable arms control agreements and their effective implementation; second, the maintenance of technological expertise in relevant weapons systems; and, third, the US remaining in Europe, so that no US President has to take the psychologically difficult step of moving troops across the Atlantic—as opposed to reinforcing those already there.

A continuing US presence in Europe is, therefore, essential. I do not believe we need to lay down specific totals. The more successful the arms process is and the greater confidence the verification process produces, the lower will be the numbers needed. I believe that a Conservative Government in the UK will pursue these policy objectives with a proper sense of history and an appropriate degree of caution, without trailing behind public expectations, where these are *legitimate*. That is the critical word. The concept of a peace dividend—which is well worth seeking—must not be thought to mean scrapping defence investment altogether.

In today's new and hopeful situation, important questions arise regarding Germany's relationship with NATO. It is for the new Germany alone ultimately to decide how she wishes to dispose her defence and security requirements. But the maintenance of confidence must be the prerequisite—for the new Germany's sake, for her neighbours, and for the Soviet Union. I offer some thoughts as to how this might be achieved, given German consent. A new—and reduced—NATO presence should remain as now, to the west of the former inner German border. The regular forces of the combined German army can remain committed to NATO, with its units deployed as before. The present West German (FRG) reserve army structure—which is not dedicated to NATO—might be developed, together with a successor to the *Bundesgrenzschutz*—West Germany's border and customs unit— and be available to be deployed *throughout* the new Germany in numbers carefully calculated not to cause alarm to her neighbours. I would argue for a continuing presence of observers, including Russians, throughout the former GDR.

I am certain the UK and France will, quite properly, wish to maintain their independent nuclear deterrents. I would expect to see a greater degree of co-operation between those two countries in nuclear capability. But we must continue to ensure that there are bases for US deterrent forces to support their European commitment. That does not preclude a discussion about the nature of those nuclear weapons, and such a dialogue has already taken place about short-range land-based nuclear weapons in the Federal Republic of Germany. It is not the precise weapons systems that now preoccupy us. It is the issue of principle involved in an effective nuclear linkage with conventional forces that is at the heart of the matter.

But there is a wider change. Not only must we strive for a re-shaped western alliance to take us into the next century. Within the new order in Europe there is an interest which could increasingly unite the two European superpowers—if I can so describe the association of western European states and the Soviet Union. As both depend greatly on stability being achieved in the emerging central European democracies, is it not possible through the continuing arms negotiations to aim for a comprehensive European treaty, binding the continent of Europe itself into a new security regime to underpin our common interests? And should we not address how we might create Europe-wide peace-keeping forces, capable of contributing towards the United Nations' efforts, and perhaps institutionalise the dialogue about matters such as the European environment, the democratic rights of citizens, the resolution of boundary disputes and other pressing matters? The NATO alliance still provides the best framework within which to negotiate such a realistic regime from our side; but as the major European players in this arrangement are common to both NATO and the European Community—whose interests are so vitally affected—it will become increasingly impossible to disentangle the two.

In this context, in the middle of 1990 I set out my views on how western Europe might react to a Middle Eastern conflict and NATO's role in such an event. At the time I pointed out the need for a Europe-wide force capable of contributing towards the United Nation's peace-keeping efforts and the long-term, potential threats which should focus the anxieties of the NATO alliance—in particular the more fanatical advocates of Muslim fundamentalism who understand with simple clarity the focusing and unifying potential of the Holy War. I said I did not, myself, foresee scope for agreement within western Europe—either within the Western European Union or the NATO alliance, and certainly not within any trans-European agreement—over out-of-area priorities; not that individual nations would not come together at moments of their choosing to intervene where they perceived their interests are at stake. But I did not feel that there were any circumstances in which the NATO alliance would act out-of-area, other than in a peace-keeping role, and that that in itself was extremely unlikely. I could not have predicted at the time how quickly these random thoughts would be exposed to the harsh light of reality.

But no one can be satisfied with the coherence—or lack of it—of the European response to the Gulf crisis, varying as it has from a British and French willingness to be involved realistically, but strictly on a national basis, to contributions from other European powers that in no sense represented their national interests in the issues at stake. The US remains firmly in the driving seat for the very obvious reason that no European response entitles it to anything but a fringe influence on policy. There are lessons to be learnt here and, if the Gulf crisis has hastened that process, then that at least would be of some benefit.

It is to be hoped that the crisis in the Gulf will not stretch out over years, although some of its consequences inevitably will. This raises two long-term problems that we shall need to address. How do democratic societies maintain the motivation and morale of their armed forces at a time when the perceived threat is very low? The demand for skilled, motivated people is growing; the supply is diminishing. The interchange between sophisticated industrial processes and the skills necessary to manage and operate militarily sophisticated weapons puts an increasing premium on the value of the personnel for whom both sectors will compete. It will tax the ingenuity of the democracies to attract people of the right calibre, even for the reduced scale of tomorrow's forces.

Equally, those anxious to consume the peace dividend will be reluctant to maintain the technologies of military deterrence. For the Europeans, with their essentially nationally-based defence arrangements, the cost of remaining credible will prove increasingly difficult to bear; and yet the time-scales for the development of modern weapons systems—a decade or more, as they often are—make it impossible to countenance the prospect of recovery, once capability has been abandoned. Realistically, there is only one desirable insurance against this, and that is enhanced co-operation in defence procurement by the nations of western Europe. Progress has been made; the coming of the single European market and the rationalisation and merger of Europe's military companies will intensify this process. But the will of the customer, that is governments, will be the determining factor.

The NATO alliance has produced its primary objective: the winning of the Cold War. Essentially, it was an alliance born of closed options, forced upon us. We now move to a world in which the options are wider, and in many ways more difficult to get right. I do not believe that we should for one moment allow the enormous progress and cohesion in the second half of the 20th century in western Europe to be fragmented and frittered away, or that the partnership for peace that straddles the Atlantic should be put at risk.

These concerns are well rehearsed in this book. They stand out with great clarity from the wide background against which they have rightly been traced.

1

Unfinished Business

'Our central theme should be the accommodation and protection of diversity within a framework . . . in which a large array of political groupings can exist, each with its own perhaps eccentric way.'

PAUL NITZE

As always, there is more history in the making than lies behind us, and reports of the 'death of history', circulating in the United States soon after the recent reversals of communism, have been greatly exaggerated. Judged by the pace of current events, history is still a sprightly young athlete. The trouble today, as the psychologist R D Laing has put it, is that change is so speeded up that we begin to see the present only when it is already disappearing.

From that difficulty in perception stem great uncertainties. Not unnaturally, these affect the debate on how the West should react to the incalculable grace that has befallen it, and the opportunities that now beckon. At its simplest it is between those who believe that our resolve in spirit and in arms has brought us victory and should therefore be maintained; and others for whom peace demands a different stance, notably the generosity and flexibility to make partners of former enemies. A world of friends, they believe, is a safer world. It is the difference between the victors at Versailles and their descendants who, a generation later, built a constructive peace in western Europe which has proved itself capable even of thawing out the Cold War.

Not unexpectedly, views in the East—and especially in the Soviet Union—are equally divided. Driven by growing economic chaos, the reformers are anxious not merely to emulate the West but to draw it into such a web of linkages as will buy both time and security. The old guard, on the other hand, remains deeply suspicious of western intentions as well as of reformist inroads on its traditional preserves. Reverses elsewhere, such as Afghanistan, have strengthened the case of the reformers by demonstrating the futility of military expenditures. But they have also stiffened the resolve of their opponents who fear that further withdrawals can easily break the morale of Soviet forces altogether, leaving the country without an effective fighting force.

Against this background the West is required urgently to adapt its policies and review its strategy. In the front line of considerations is the NATO alliance, the visible and effective symbol of the West's determination to defend its freedoms and to resist all forms of attack upon it. Its rationale was the threat from the East. When that has been removed, can NATO still be relevant? The preamble to the North Atlantic Treaty declares that the parties are determined to preserve their common heritage and the civilisation of their peoples which rest upon the principles of democracy, individual freedom and the rule of law. Once the main protagonists in eastern Europe base themselves on the same principles of democracy and human rights, what further need of opposing blocs and alliances?

There has been much discussion of transforming NATO into a primarily political body, whilst retaining and reorientating its defensive capacity. Perhaps this is to overlook the obvious fact that NATO has always been a political organisation: the physical expression of the political commitment of its sixteen members. Yet change there must be. The basic problems are twofold: determining the direction of that change; and weathering the transition from here to there, bearing in mind that in military terms transition is the most sensitive manoeuvre of all. Before contemplating any such moves, we need to see clearly where we stand and be sure that, as far as humanly possible, we have defined the right objectives.

Our times in the making

In 1917 the Romanov throne crumbled under the deprivations of the First World War. For eight months, the Moscow spring took over from centuries of Tsarist repression and disdain for the humanity of its subjects. Seventy years later, the Leninist commissars who usurped that revolution had also to give way in the face of economic blight. A society bled white by the senseless ambition to become a military superpower had once more turned upon itself. Decades of repression and denial of democracy in that vast empire east of the 'Iron Curtain' had finally led to popular uprisings, the overthrow of Leninist doctrine, the discarding of Marxist orthodoxies, and the instituting of democratic—if not yet pluralist—elections.

Without firing a single shot, the steadfastness of the NATO alliance had achieved its major aim. For the men in the Kremlin, its demonstrable unity and cohesion had made it a determined adversary. The sacrifices of the sixteen NATO members and their peoples in maintaining the ultimate in preparedness had also ensured that the race for supremacy became intolerably expensive. For a rare moment in history, possession of a full armoury and a readied war machine had not inexorably led to war.

Yet these were not the only factors. The compulsion on Mr Gorbachev to liberalise was one thing; the confidence that the USSR could safely weaken its defences without being attacked by an alliance for so long held up as the imperialist enemy was quite another. Parallel political developments in western Europe undoubtedly played a significant role.

Seen from Moscow, the European Community (EC) has wrought a profound transformation not only in the standard of living of its members but in the potential threat of any renewed aggression. Its achievement has been to create a reluctant superpower without nationalism, without external ambitions—yet with enough economic power to offer both an example and urgent help for the USSR's problems.

The EC's major achievement, however, must have been seen as the assimilation of West Germany (FRG). It is today politically unthinkable that any EC member should embark on a passage of arms with its neighbours. More than that, it has become economically and militarily impossible for anyone to do so: economically because, since Robert Schuman and the Coal and Steel Community, European heavy industry and its supplies have been deliberately scrambled to be wholly interdependent; militarily because NATO is able to exercise restraint on its members as well as to mobilise them for concerted action. A highly specific restraint is that West Germany is unable to possess nuclear weapons or use its forces independently of NATO.

The Soviet Union thus found itself with its historic enemy both partitioned and neutralised. At the same time, co-operation in place of confrontation with the new Europe and the United States became an imperative for economic reasons. The Soviet people would no longer tolerate the shortages imposed on them in the interests of a constant state of alert.

Seen from the West, the change—however welcome and exceeding our wildest hopes—has replaced fear and rigidity with flux and instability. There is much talk of balkanisation, of suppressed nationalities seeking revenge and fragmenting into mini-states. The greater danger is from hitherto silenced minorities rediscovering an identity and demanding a voice. Such frictions may spring as easily from 'states' within the USSR as from ethnic pockets yearning to be reunited with some neighbouring homeland.

There is now a clear need to neutralise such conflicts, to requite these ambitions within a new form of governance. The EC may already have shown us a model for a centripetal political order, one which gives countries a reason for coming together rather than splintering apart. There may well be others to be found. What is clear is that we need to build an open, transnational society in which power is diffused and the significance of borders reduced.

Until we have developed a vision of what the Europe of tomorrow will need to defend, and mapped the threats to be contained, it will be difficult to design a security system that meets our needs. The long years of the Cold War have shown us that peace is more than the absence of war. They have also demonstrated that we need a holistic approach to security which rests not only on military resolve but also on our political, economic and social strength. If peace is indivisible, so too is security.

The Revolution of 1989

Millions of us watched with emotion as the people of East Berlin breached the Wall, breaking out of their prison and reuniting East with West in a thousand spontaneous embraces. Our hearts leapt as we watched the Ceauşescus flee the wrath of the people they had for so long enchained and exploited. Throughout the greater half of the European continent, we saw the courage of desperation suddenly triumph over decades of humiliation imposed in the name of communism. How did it happen?

Some of the causes will form part of living experience and be easily identified. The advent of Mr Gorbachev in 1985 in the Soviet Union, the progressive establishment of his benevolent physiognomy bearing witness to the new tablets of *glasnost* and *perestroika*, culminating in raptures of Gorbymania (and Raisamania); the rise of Poland's Lech Walesa and the birth of *Solidarnosz* in the Gdansk shipyards; the return of Pope Woytila to his Polish flock, kissing the ground from which only a short time ago he had been elevated to Rome.

Yet these are only the most visible, easily remembered landmarks on a road whose beginnings stretch into a historical distance down to the birth of the memories, concepts and prejudices with which those peoples and their leaders are imbued today. From there date the springs of today's revolution; there also we must seek the key to some of the current problems yet to be negotiated. Without a realisation of what motivates those with whom we will from now on be dealing in great intimacy, we shall be unable to win the trust which needs to be at the heart of future accords.

Although often hidden from all but the historian, there are layers of sensitivities which we shall ignore at our peril. History has a habit of leaving loose ends to snare successor generations, unseen banana skins for them to slide to sudden perdition. How deep in the Soviet subconscious lies the fact that only in 1945 was she able to recapture the last pieces of the huge tracts of white Russia and the western Ukraine taken from her in the 13th and 14th centuries?

Here also may lie an explanation why the 1989 Revolution, whose root causes appear identical from Berlin to Tbilisi, is so far from uniform in its effects. The German Democratic Republic (GDR) has become one with its former arch-enemy, the Federal Republic of Germany. Poland, Hungary, Czechoslovakia are once again fully-fledged democracies, even if their economies have still to be liberalised. The Baltic states—Estonia, Latvia, Lithuania—have declared similar ambitions, delayed only because, fifty years ago, they were swallowed up into the Soviet Union.

Further east, however, the changes become less clear. Although the particular tyranny of Ceauşescu had gone, Romanian elections produced little change in method; the party seems again to rule under another name. In Bulgaria the result is ambivalent. Albania lies on the razor's edge. And what of the great Soviet Union itself? In the face of imminent break-up from secession of its outlying republics, faced once more, as in 1917, with the prospect of famine and food strikes, its leaders cling to the only stability they know—the Communist Party. Pluralism is still facing its hardest test in the heartland of the original Revolution.

What is the cement which still binds that tottering edifice? And how is it that the Communist Party, universally despised by the people, still holds sway? The fear of disintegration certainly is one explanation. The slide into chaos, a fracturing into small and helpless nationalities, fissures along ethnic and fundamentalist divisions, must strike terror into most hearts. Moves towards local economic autonomy, the domestic equivalent of former Soviet foreign minister Shevardnadze's 'Sinatra doctrine' of everybody doing it their way, are an acknowledgement that the leadership is sensitive to the storm raging around it; yet at the same time it has lashed itself firmly to the Party mast.

One key lies in the need to differentiate between the impulses for human rights and for democracy. It was the human rights movement which broke the fetters. Newly won democracy then brought people the ability to form fresh bonds with those closest to them and their ideals. Hence the initial fruits of democracy are a multiplicity of parties and separatist factions. Fortunately, in the three westernmost countries, solid majorities have emerged to make political democracy and government viable. In the Soviet Union those factions remain within the one party. The real test has still to come, once the Communist Party allows rivals on to the scene.

Even limited elections within the one-party system have already produced the outlines of groups which can readily splinter into separate political organisations. On the other hand, rivalries between individual republics are plain and in the open. The Soviet leadership is facing the choice between the sanctity of the Party and the survival of the Union. A democratic pluralist system of all-Soviet parties may yet serve to keep the republics joined in a looser federation, allowing for greater local autonomy. The alternative can only be progressive disintegration—or the reimposition of centralist authority with some measure of force.

The German factor

Such are the nightmares besetting the leaders in the Kremlin. But there are others. Undoubtedly the second most pressing is the future of Germany. Ironically, just as the Soviet Union finds itself hobbled by threatened dismemberment, West Germany (FRG) has gained strength through unification with what, until recently, constituted an outlying province of the Soviet empire. Unease about Germany runs deep in the Soviet consciousness. Two world wars were fought on Soviet soil, in which lie buried countless millions of soldiers and civilians. Hitler's war in the East was as brutal as it was treacherous, and suspicion has been kept alive throughout the Cold War.

Two factors conspire to aggravate that unease. The first is the physical weakening and ultimate loss of forward defensive positions in eastern Germany. Even now these have to be supplied across Polish territory whose reliability as both transit and buffer zone must be in doubt. Secondly, the whole relationship between Germany and the USSR is one of ambivalence. Despite forty years of exemplary West German behaviour, politically as well as democratically, and twenty years of 'Ostpolitik', suspicion has not been laid completely to rest.

If the regression of Soviet hostility can have a single cause, it must be not just the West's undoubted determination to stand firm, but the efforts of successive West German chancellors, from Adenauer's visit in 1955 onwards. From 1969 Willy Brandt's Ostpolitik gave a bold signal that the West would countenance friendly relations and extend the hand of economic co-operation. With it went trade and substantial loan financing, secured by the 1970 Moscow treaty. Yet it still took several years before Leonid Brezhnev finally felt able to set foot in Bonn.

Today, no one imagines that Germany would ever launch a military attack upon the Soviet Union. Even hardliners will have seen the total impossibility of that. But any accommodations—such as a unified Germany's position in NATO—which simply increase Germany's strategic position without some compensating reassurances for Moscow are just not practical politics in today's environment. The already formidable opposition facing Mr Gorbachev would have made decisive extra capital out of the German bogey-man.

At the same time the USSR is conscious that it needs Germany, both for its economic strength and as a reliable political partner in the years to come.

There were also some misgivings about German unification in the west. Clearly the fear is that, as the largest country in Europe outside the USSR, and certainly the most dynamic, its economy will rapidly dominate all others. Not for the first time there are mutterings about deutschmark diplomacy.

Instinctive Soviet fears of German economic expansionism are undoubtedly as inchoate as anyone else's—including those good burghers in East Germany who now find themselves part of the German economy. Yet Germany has been the economic dynamo of the European Community. If now we are about to create a wider Europe, its powerhouse will need a commensurately bigger turbine. Much of the power will, over the early years, be syphoned off for east European reconstruction, requiring an effort every bit as great and urgent as the Marshall Plan on which the rehabilitation of the western part of the continent depended after 1945. Yet even that may cause tensions.

The United States will be the first to know how power, affluence and a universally desired currency can buy as much unpopularity as respect. Inferiority complexes are quick to grow, even among friends and allies. Psychologically, it may be that US intervention in Europe became responsible for creating that sense of distinctiveness which so suddenly led to the finding of a European identity—and thence to the formation of the EC—only the briefest span after the cessation of the murderous hostilities in Europe.

Half a century ago, Germany sundered Europe. Today we have the chance to use her to make Europe whole again. After forty years of apology and reparations to Israel and the West, she is now willing to treat also with the rest of those she had wronged. But the price may be some recognition that the slate of atrocities has been wiped clean by subsequent revenge. Reconciliation is not to forget the past, but the effort to build a common future by learning from it.

The outlines of a new Europe

What the forty-five years of the post-war era have witnessed is the progressive bridging of incompatibilities, enmities and rivalries within a web of contractual arrangements. Unlike the treaties of former times, however, each one required its signatories to yield a piece of sovereignty as an earnest. The North Atlantic Treaty, signed in 1949, was the first and most decisive derogation of sovereignty: the principle of an attack on one being an attack on all partially removed from national competence the decision to go to war. If the system was notably successful, it was because it acted as a deterrent on both the potential outside aggressor and on any adventurer there might have been in its midst.

Since 1958 the European Community has gone further. Beginning with a pooling of trade policy towards the outside world, the Community's remit has touched upon every field of social, political and economic affairs. Plans for an early economic and monetary union have entered their first phase; currencies are linked and all remaining internal obstacles to Community-wide movement of people, goods and capital will shortly disappear. With them will go the frontiers over which so much blood has been spilled through the centuries. Political union, with common foreign policies and some form of security dimension, has already moved firmly onto the agenda.

Western Europe, in short, has made remarkable strides not just in economic terms but in finding an underlying political unity. The logic of the enterprise begun by no more than six states has driven it forward to an extent where it has often surprised itself. The Community has doubled its membership and has applications pending from countries like Austria and Turkey. It has an outer ring of countries belonging to the European Free Trade Area—once regarded by the United Kingdom as an alternative pattern—with which it has entered into an economic association. Effectively the whole of western Europe, neutrals and NATO members alike, belongs to or is linked with the European Community.

Since 1986, when the USSR formally recognised the EC, trade agreements have been completed with all the Comecon countries, including the USSR itself. Only weeks after the installation of their newly elected governments, all the smaller east European states applied for Community membership. For the time being, the Community has offered them association agreements; negotiations are already advanced with Bulgaria, Czechoslovakia, Hungary and Poland. Delegations of the Commission have been opened in Budapest, Warsaw and Moscow.

The time is clearly ripe for the extension of the 'Community method' to the new states of eastern Europe. Association with a democratic and peaceable pole of growth is in itself desirable. Much more important, however, is the adoption of the mechanisms of pooled sovereignty by countries which will never need stability more than they do now. That can be done with or without full membership of the EC, voluntarily among themselves or as a pre-condition of eventual accession. Since full membership is likely to be some years away, it is heartening to see the initiative taken by Italy within the 'Pentagonale' to expand economic and political ties with Austria, Czechoslovakia, Hungary, Poland and Yugoslavia. From the Adriatic to the Baltic, a new area of regional co-operation is in the making.

There are several reasons why EC membership may not at this stage supply the best solution. Although the USSR has finally—but only recently—brought itself to recognise the EC and entertain relations with it, a wholesale defection from Comecon into the arms of the EC would be viewed with some misgivings. Even if not of the same consequence as if eastern Europe went over straight from Warsaw Pact to NATO, it would increase the USSR's unease about the permanent tilt of the balance of power. No degree of persuasion that the extra stability on its borders would only be beneficial could counteract the additional feeling of isolation from seeing erstwhile allies irrevocably switching sides.

The first requirement of a permanently stable solution throughout a new Europe is to abolish precisely that view of opposing 'sides'—the bloc mentality. For more than forty years the continent has been divided into two opposing power blocs, facing each other in full panoply across the iron curtain. The greatest service we can do to ourselves is to acknowledge that those days are over. True that the USSR remains the largest single military force in Europe. Equally true that its internal instability makes it as dangerous and unpredictable as a rusty unexploded bomb—and a nuclear one at that. Yet its own power bloc has dissolved, its economy can no longer be mobilised onto a war footing or its people motivated to fight. What threat remains is not from an integrated superpower but from the instability of a disintegrating supernova.

This realisation is crucial to every aspect of the new international system we have now to design and construct. We need to begin by revising our own view of the world. Nothing will ever again fit into the neat compartments with which we have lived for two generations. Stereotypes of goodies and baddies, cowboys and Indians, friend and foe, have been relegated to the past. Just as the pillars of classical science have given way to the uncertainty principle of sub-atomic physics, so our political map is likely to be one of overlapping systems, ordered in a kind of creative instability. Membership of these may well be random: some states belonging to one but not another, depending on geography and purpose. The countries of central Europe, after all, have their cultural affinities with the West, though for the time being linked politically with the East.

Centralism has become discredited. In the West it has been the cause of all our major wars. In the East it served as the instrument of oppression and colonisation. Both East and West are today voluntarily assuming looser bonds of governance. The Soviet Union has relaxed its control over the economic policies of its individual republics, and may be forced to yield more within a lightly fitting federation. The EC is firmly wedded to its 'principle of subsidiarity', which in Community-speak means that only those competences which cannot be exercised at a lower level are transferred upwards.

In between, eastern Europe also needs a new structure into which to fit. Not just the new democracies, but possibly also the outer Soviet republics will be looking for somewhere to go, even whilst staying politically within a kind of 'Red Commonwealth'. If it is too early for EC membership, an institutionalised Conference on Security and Co-operation in Europe (CSCE) can provide the right venue.

We have now identified three characteristics for a new construction: a productive framework for a unified Germany, an end to the bloc system, and a pooling of sovereignty. There are others. It should lend itself to continual adaptation, as circumstances arise which we cannot as yet predict. It should ensure that the Soviet Union feels neither isolated nor threatened; it should actively involve all three superpowers—the USA, USSR and now the EC. Above all, it should be capable of permanence.

A new Concert of Europe

Two world wars have surged across Europe and over Russian soil this century. Both ended in a fragile peace, yet the Soviet Union had no part in the settlements. In 1919 the Treaty of Versailles was made without them, and their absence heavily affected its terms. No formal peace treaty crowned the allied victory in 1945, since the shooting war was rapidly succeeded by the Cold War. So, far from the USSR playing a role in the ordering of peaceful relationships, on both occasions dispositions had to be made to contain them as much as the former enemy. Thus for the Soviet Union there has been no formal end to either world war. Until the signing of the 1990 Treaty of Good Neighbourliness, Protection and Co-operation, the Tannenberg Armistice of 1917 may well have represented the sole instrument for the cessation of hostilities between the USSR and Germany. The 1921 Rapallo agreement, as well as the Moscow treaty of 1970, though attempts to normalise relations, were essentially pacts of convenience, dealing only with isolated parts of the whole relationship.

The time for peace treaties now lies in the past. But it seems none too soon, and not too late, to aim at a comprehensive settlement between all the former belligerents—effectively the whole of Europe aside from the handful of countries which managed to remain aloof from the conflict. Never has there been such an opportunity for building a new world. Past concordats have invariably been between exhausted victors and demoralised vanquished, wanting to put an end to yesterday but lacking the vision for tomorrow.

Only twice in modern history has an international conclave tried to build peace in Europe. The first time, the major protagonists at the Concert of Europe in 1815—Britain, Russia, Austria and Prussia— tried to create a new order out of the legacy of the Napoleonic wars. In a sense they, too, thought they had vanquished not only the heir to the French Revolution but also the dangerous ideas proclaimed by the

Communes of Paris. The Quadruple Alliance and the peace of Vienna were therefore as much about frontiers as about the creation of a bulwark against the new liberalism. Inevitably, ideas in the end proved stronger than proscriptions, and led to renewed tensions, especially among the peacemakers themselves.

Much less enlightened were the victors of the First World War, assembled at Versailles in 1919. True, US President Wilson's ambition to create 'the perpetual alliance of democratic peoples in a League of Nations dedicated to peace' had the mark of greatness; yet his failure to commit the USA to becoming a member caused it to be born with a fatal weakness which eventually proved its undoing. The severity of reparations imposed on Germany helped also to create an injustice which soon became the focus for the new, virulent nationalism which finally propelled Europe and the Atlantic world into its second great conflict.

Blunders were also made further east. Significantly, the historian H A L Fisher writes, 'Later it would seem that the Big Three of Versailles had made a bad mistake in not imposing economic federation on the states which had inherited the ruins of Austro-Hungary.'[1] Those states—Czechoslovakia, Hungary, Yugoslavia—are precisely those on which attention is focused today. Seventy years on, now joined by Poland, they are trying to redress some of those mistakes within the Pentagonale.

History has thus helped us to repair two of those former omissions. In our age small nations are no longer afraid to recognise their need to work together in ways which are selective but binding. And our achievement is to have constructed an Atlantic alliance in which the USA is, this time, a full and permanent member.

Today we also have the chance to build a settlement with honour on all sides, and without the vengeance which marked Versailles. In our time there is no victor, no vanquished, and no diktat for one to impose upon the other. Despite the understandable elation of those who held the line and stiffened our resolve to resort to arms if the need arose, we have not won the cold war. Victory, if there was one, belongs to the peoples of eastern Europe who took to the streets and defied their oppressors. It belongs to their sacrifices at least as much as ours, for theirs were by far the greater. When was there ever an age when the walls of the prison crumbled from within, when the prisoners could walk freely from darkness to liberty, from poverty to the chance eventually to participate in the abundance of the western table?

Half a century later, no longer with the hot pride of victory, we can consider a wise and lasting peace. We have had time to reach political maturity, to abandon notions of supremacy because we now know its price, and to develop new institutions appropriate to our concerns. Without passion, we can look at past errors and incompetence and avoid the fatal flaws which enmity and prejudice caused us to build into our endeavours.

The Congress of Vienna was also an attempt to balance Germany. Although disposing of small parcels of real estate, it attempted an agreed all-European design for what it thought of as the post-Napoleonic age. Today we need to ask ourselves if our aim is to create such a design, or whether we are content with small repairs to the old bipolar system. If we do not mourn the semblance of security derived from that bipolarity, we can indeed keep alive the lofty ideals of a new Concert of Europe, this time devoted to the protection rather than the repression of liberal development.

Elements of the new concordat

What then would such a new settlement embrace?

The principal impulse must be to end the climate of confrontation, to dissolve the divisions among opposing blocs, and to build confidence in the peaceable intentions of all partners to the new compact.

This will inevitably entail modifications to the two now very unequal alliances; these will be discussed in a later chapter. Soon to go into liquidation, the Warsaw Pact exists with little more military reality than its name. But it has seen service as a useful bargaining counter and a screen behind which its former allies were able to negotiate matters which could not immediately be treated with the West. NATO has seen the opposite problem. It remains a highly effective military pact which will find it more difficult by far to reduce its strength and adopt a more convincingly peaceable role.

The second objective must be to fortify such a new climate with the reality of peace. Above all that means creating conditions where conflict becomes the less preferred solution because it is seen to bring only losses and no gains. Eradication of conflict will never be achieved by decree. The political, and particularly ethnic, volatility of many of the newly enfranchised countries will offer a host of problems and frictions. The only practical solution is to make keeping the peace so rewarding, and the resort to violence so unattractive, as to induce an automatic stability.

If punitive threats are no longer to have a place in the new Europe, rewards for keeping within the law have to be achieved solely by economic means. That argues for a programme of economic aid and linkages akin to those developed in western Europe since 1945.

Some of these are already in place: the World Bank has set aside over US$2 billion a year for a substantial programme in eastern Europe; the 24 OECD countries under the leadership of the EC were quick to co-ordinate immediate relief for Poland and Hungary, now extended to others; and the new European Bank for Reconstruction and Development has been formally established with an endowment of US$12 billion. An important task will be to relate this assistance to progress not only in adopting economic systems within which funds can be used to best advantage, but also in entering into close and inextricable economic co-operation with their neighbours. Spectres of exploitation within Comecon will have to be buried, interred with Comecon itself.

But it takes two to make a war. Should there then also be a system of guarantees for countries against aggression by others? Disintegration of the Warsaw Pact has effectively removed from them the unwanted protection of the Soviet Union. NATO cannot replace that for them without being seen as opportunist and striking war-like postures. All eyes are currently on the Conference on Security and Co-operation in Europe (CSCE). Known as the 'Helsinki process', it looks like the framework within which an answer must eventually be found. Its now 34 members include all countries of Europe (with the present exception of Albania), together with the USA and Canada. A major task will be to build up trust in this process and in its eventual capacity to arbitrate between potential belligerents. The new countries of eastern Europe must be given the reassurance that it will become a co-operative system capable of reducing their present exposure.

The superpowers have become too powerful to operate in this European space. Their nuclear arms may still be necessary to deter each other, to give each one the comfort of knowing that the risks faced by the other are too great for him to be tempted to attack. But the only effective weapon capable of being deployed on European soil will from now on be diplomacy. In this, Europe will continue to be vitally dependent on US involvement. The solidarity of the Atlantic alliance will continue to be a crucial aspect of European diplomacy, putting the grip into the diplomatic handshake. But its military significance will inevitably be reduced as the confidence building process becomes established and gradually takes over the role of guaranteeing the peace from the military function.

This is not to suggest building the new Europe on the illusion of pacifism or neutralism. Quite the contrary. NATO, the US connection, even the bomb, are by turns the cause and the result of the West's prosperity. Their co-operation, born of the dire-seeming threat, has taught them other ways of pursuing a common endeavour. Recognition of their interdependence led on to the EC, the OECD, the North American Free Trade Area, and many other collaborative enterprises. All were based on free and voluntary co-operation, none on coercion. All in their various ways can serve as models for the kind of structures on which to build the wider Europe. They are capable of laying the foundations for what Sir Michael Howard, Professor of Military and Naval History at Yale University, has described as a European Commonwealth.

A remarkable feature of the present time is the close identity of terms in which Soviet and western leaders describe their respective visions of that Europe. Not only was Chancellor Adenauer's simile of a 'European house' echoed across the years by President Gorbachev's call for a 'common European home'; both sides see institutionalising the Helsinki process as the way forward, and with it the permanent involvement of the USA in European affairs.

The Charter of Paris signed by the 34 nations has set up a standing secretariat to service it. Its governing body is a Council of Foreign Ministers, with subsidiary tiers of ministers and officials at working level. There is agreement on a centre for the prevention of conflict between its members, endowed with mechanisms for verification. Most significant of all, the Charter acknowledges the continuation of NATO by endorsing the freedom of states to choose their own security arrangements.

Finally, a European settlement must set a frame for a united Germany. Its economic and political weight must be harnessed to European reconstruction. Even if the number of its *Länder* has increased by five, its population by 16 million and its armed forces by whatever is left after wholesale defections from the Nationale Volksarmee, that does not need to alarm the USSR. Germany has already pledged itself to voluntary limitation on the size of its armed forces. In addition, the conventional armed forces reduction treaty imposes an automatic levelling on any increase in NATO potential acquired in this or any other way; and the Soviet Union will be in a position to monitor it.

Stripped of that bogey, German unification must be seen as a plus factor, as a leaven to stimulate fresh thinking and new relationships. The coming together of the two German peoples raised under opposing ideologies is a reconciliation for the whole of Europe. East German relationships with their former allies will fructify the West and aid mutual contacts and understanding. The economic success which is likely in the formerly impoverished GDR will be a demonstration to give hope and encouragement to all the eastern economies awaiting their own rehabilitation.

The startling lesson of the Cold War has been that there are no military solutions, only economic ones. Political standing, the capacity to negotiate and achieve one's international objectives, social policies, in short everything that a nation needs to do depends fundamentally on its economic strength. If its own becomes insufficient, it must achieve it jointly with its neighbours. The new settlement, and the new Europe must be based on economic reality. If peace is to be a lasting component, then it too must be built on economic equity.

Had that been recognised at Versailles or at Yalta, much pain could conceivably have been spared. With that new awareness, now is the time for us to conclude the business left unfinished at the last joint meeting of the allied victors in Potsdam.

For the third time this century, we have the opportunity to develop a framework for international security. Its contours may be those of a European Community from Brest to Brest-Litovsk, and a security system from Vancouver to Vladivostok. Not only must we not miss it for a third time, but we must do it before proliferation elsewhere denies us the chance.

2

The Extension of Diplomacy

'War is the continuation of policy by other means. It is not merely a political act, but a real political instrument.'

CLAUSEWITZ

. . . is more diplomacy

Since 1945—as Raymond Aron has pointed out—and for the first time in history, the great powers have been preparing for a war they did not wish to fight.[2] It follows that the classical Clausewitz option was not open to them. The war that seemed to loom would not be of their volition but of their opponent's. Hence it was no longer their political instrument, but one that could only be used against them.

Why had history changed to our disadvantage? Although ravaged by the Second World War, the western economy was still strong. Within a remarkably short time western Europe had recovered, old enmities healed and co-operative economic and military efforts launched. Never had there been an arsenal of such devastating power and credibility. Never before had peacetime planning succeeded in creating so formidable a battle array. Why then was the West deprived of the age-old extension of diplomacy?

The answer lies precisely in the strength of that arsenal. The nuclear bomb had changed the world. Its unimaginable power, carefully nurtured and escalated to make the incinerators of Hiroshima and Nagasaki look like harmless firecrackers, had made it a weapon to keep the peace, no longer to fight a war. Its awesome power could destroy not only the enemy target, but in time the launcher's own environment. Even if he could interdict retaliation with a first strike, his own children would slowly perish in the nuclear winter.

17

Only now that the threat has receded are we beginning to see the kind of world we have lived in for two whole generations. The nuclear debate has gone back and forth, washing over us without our being capable of the effort of imagination to follow its logic. Most people are incapable of envisaging real horror more dramatic than a Hammer movie. At a certain point the imagination becomes deadened and refuses to make the final leap into insanity. Even anti-nuclear campaigners were unable to go beyond the moral ground of the pacifist and paint in humanity's ultimate obscenity.

Are our nuclear deterrents then akin to the Emperor's clothes? Has almost everyone been afraid to speak up and say that they had no reality, that their gain in destructive mass had cost them their substance? No, for that kind of truth is visible to the majority only in retrospect. It is the sudden illumination that comes with any narrow escape.

To have seen it once, however, alters one's view for all time. From now on the continuation of diplomacy must be more diplomacy. Diplomacy must indeed develop other means, but war is no longer one of them. If all-out war is now the unthinkable result of the failure of diplomacy, it presents us with a wholly new challenge. Napoleon held that diplomacy was the police in grand costume. That may be even truer now than for his time, for we have disarmed our police and not even a truncheon can be seen dangling suggestively from their belt. So where diplomatists fail, politicians and summits have now to be brought in.

But has exposure of the fiction cost us our deterrent? Miraculous as it would be if we had succeeded in abolishing war, are we not once more delivered into the uncertainties which marked the pre-nuclear age, at the mercy of predators and others' insanities? If so, we would have lost all and gained only a temporary respite until our adversary had reconstructed his economy and renewed his ability to wage war.

Here too we must adjust our sights to newly-found realities. Our great discovery is not that war is impossible; it is that we can no longer win it. The lesson is that, as President Mitterrand of France at the London Summit in July 1990 put it, 'The purpose of defence is to prevent a war, not to win a war.' To the determined aggressor, therefore, it remains open to use lethal force. It remains open to us to resist it, with whatever means available. So long as either side suspects that this could involve the nuclear option, we continue to have a deterrent.

What is important, therefore, is the nuclear uncertainty, the belief that nuclear arms *may* be used in given circumstances, and that war-like acts on any scale *may* provoke such a response. The real deterrent lies not in the nuclear warheads themselves, but in the use of that conditional. In the post-1989 world it is no longer the steely certainty that nuclear weapons will be used against an aggressor which will continue to buy us peace, but the uncertainty that they might or might not. An essential part of our defence will continue to rest upon that uncertainty principle.

It is, however, significant that here too size has become counter-productive. The larger the arsenal, the greater the number of war-heads, the more unlikely is it that they will be unleashed for mutual destruction. It is a corollary of current agreed reductions that a new measure of credibility will attach to what remains. This continues to be the rationale behind the British and French nuclear capability.

The smallness principle does not, of course, extend to tactical or battlefield weapons. Their possession has become objectionable to both friend and foe. They engender suspicion on the part of those with whom we can now negotiate on the basis of friendship; and they repel all those, from Potsdam to Poznan, newly liberated from the fear of being the Warsaw Pact's front line, and on whose soil they would be used. Reductions in strategic warheads, and abolition of tactical weapons—along with chemical and anti-personnel devices generally––are therefore a sound and desirable response to the changed situation in Europe.

The *locus belli*, the theatre in which one could envisage serious hostilities, has itself acquired a different dimension. Is it a serious contribution to those newly enfranchised states of eastern Europe to maintain a defence strategy that still designates them as a potential battleground? Surely our strategy must be to show that the West is not a bloc—such as that from which they have only lately escaped—which steamrollers small countries for its own interests, but rather itself a group of free peoples welcoming them in voluntary association. Unless our planning is radically and demonstrably changed, we shall betray them and undermine our own enhanced security.

There are therefore further reasons why war, with its implied nuclear dimension, has ceased to be a viable option. One is simply that we have run out of space. This is not only because the Warsaw Pact has effectively shrunk and, were the USSR still to be the notional aggressor, the line of transgression would now lie a thousand kilometres further east. The main reason is that the territory covered by our moral protection has moved correspondingly forward. The distance from that new line to Moscow is roughly equivalent to the depth of the new territory it delimits. It is even more unthinkable that nuclear warheads could be despatched against targets virtually in our backyard.

By the same token it is, of course, imperative that we should protect them also against any counter-threat from the East. In the nuclear context it is not pejorative to postulate that threat as coming from the Soviet Union—even out of its disintegration—for it remains the only potential nuclear belligerent in the European theatre. That places a double responsibility on our capacity to procure peace by civil means. To achieve that will be the purpose and the challenge of the new concordat discussed above.

The genies released

The nuclear context, as we have seen, is unlikely to be the crucial one. Wars are fought for supremacy and, in the old East-West terms, the West is now unassailable. Its economic, technical and military strength can patently find no match. Even without the ultimate deterrent, the risk of a classic confrontational war has all but vanished. Yet at the same time the causes of potential minor conflicts have sharply increased. Countries which have newly gained their independence tend to be jealous of their frontiers. Worse, because of the haphazard ways of 19th-century peacemaking, state lines did not correspond with nationalities. Countries claiming a historic collectivity are not necessarily nations, but aggregations of peoples of different ethnic origins, customs and allegiances.

Soviet hegemony kept all these diversities tightly bottled up. Now that freedom has become the order of the day, such tensions have licence to express themselves. Minorities in one country may be supported in a struggle for recognition by a neighbouring country from which they were spalled off. Albanians in Serbian Kosovo, Slovenian independence and Croatian separatism within the same Yugoslav federation are creating uncontainable tensions. In the Soviet Union itself, overlapping minorities in Armenia, Khirgizia, Uzbekistan and Moldavia have rioted, whilst independence movements have sprung up not only in the Baltic states but in Georgia and in the great Republic of Russia itself. With its southern republics, the USSR will, before long, have a predominantly Islamic population, susceptible to influences from the Middle East and elsewhere.

The collapse of Soviet power has opened up opportunities for the re-emergence of historic rivalries and hatreds. Economic reform will be neither smooth nor speedy. In the short term, public expectation is likely to be severely disappointed. Newly-established democracies could founder, as public opinion opted for—or was coerced into—seeking more decisive solutions. In such circumstances people hungry for power would readily exploit any passion that was to hand. An appeal to ethnic rivalries or national instinct would in such a situation be a potent weapon.

Within a relatively short period the major west European countries will have become deeply involved economically in central Europe, as the hunger for investment draws in their larger companies. Inadequate progress towards economic reform, public frustration, and the growing influence of western commerce are further ingredients in a potential political cauldron which, here or there, could reach boiling point.

Lines of fracture abound. They add an extra element of instability to the flux in which the 1989 Revolution has left eastern Europe. Yet there is one great force for good which has been released: the respect for human rights and democratic practice. Even where communist party look-alikes have gained a majority in more or less fair elections, they have had to trim their methods to the new reality. The first freely elected Bulgarian President was swiftly ousted for talking of using tanks against demonstrators. Despite backing from battalions of rough-neck miners, events for his counterpart in a rather less reconstructed Romania may take a similar course.

We in the West who live under democratic systems, with all their weaknesses and imperfections, should be the last to delude ourselves that they offer an automatic passport to happiness. Yet the compelling force of the democratic ideal had already been demonstrated in our time against tyrants as diverse as Salazar in Portugal, Marcos in the Philippines, and a grand array of military juntas in Latin America. Most of these new democracies were created without much outside help, and most have managed to maintain themselves even in the face of heavy economic and political odds. Come to that, nearly half the membership of the EC has, in recent history, been in the grip of totalitarian regimes.

Democracy is altogether a tougher plant than we are apt to give it credit for. There should be little doubt that it will be able to maintain itself where once it has taken hold. The danger therefore is from other forces which can undermine the state; and the most real of these is the resurgent nationalism of minorities, especially when assisted from outside. The enemy of democracy is the totalitarian seeking to impose his infallibility. The enemy of national stability is the nationalism of an aggrieved minority. Curiously, enhanced democracy is the solution for both.

The West has rightly been seen as the progenitor and the bastion of democracy. From Greek antiquity to the present day we have nurtured and developed its precepts, built institutions to improve it and fought increasingly greater wars for its protection. What we have signally failed to do over 3000 years is to bring democracy into the relations between states. The United Nations notwithstanding, at this level anarchy still rules throughout most of the world. The compelling criterion in international relations is the national interest, which is seen as legitimising whatever folly or perfidy seems expeditious.

The real opportunity, the great extension of diplomacy required of us today, lies precisely in that field. If today's challenge is to move from confrontation to equity, from containment to co-operation, then it is by employing the tools and practice of democracy that we shall achieve it. Can we envisage within that confined European space a kind of parliament of nations, a forum not only for debate but for the airing of grievances, a method of righting wrongs and protecting the weak? Surely it would be just such an institution which could defuse and requite the minority problems which constitute today's threat to our security.

The democratisation of former totalitarian states has restored them to moral health. Even if still beset by the infirmities of poverty and instability, they have returned to the common family. A healthy mind in a healthy body is an apt precept also for the body politic. Just as we have seen it in our interest to aid their economic recovery, we need to find an appropriate transnational framework within which to speed their recovery. We have simultaneously to ensure that their system is not undermined by the virus of nationalism, so that they can remain immune from relapse.

What is security?

In order to appreciate the urgency of this task we need a deeper understanding of what precisely is the nature of security. Super-ficially, it must be the certainty that, at any given time, a perceived or potential threat will be balanced by the protection afforded by one's own forces and those of dependable allies. In the past we have relied on scaling up our strength as our threat perception increased. That has successfully led to the present situation. Equally, it has brought us close to the absolute limits of the arms race. The dynamic of our situation, however, goes way beyond the abatement of the threat: it also offers us one of the rare historic opportunities for *actively participating* in the full elimination of that threat.

Seen in a deeper perspective, security must ultimately rest not on wilfully feuding nations and their ad hoc alliances, but on some higher responsibility and authority. Internationally, we stand today at the point where our ancestors had to abandon private armies or posses in favour of a neutral and permanent police force. That was the age when the familiarity of the village or neighbourhood, capable of devising and applying its own justice, became absorbed into the anonymity of ever larger urban units. As populations grew more dense and less bonded, the rule of law needed a longer arm to enforce its writ.

The closer people live together, the greater their need for security. The stresses of urban life often demand protection from, rather than by, one's neighbours. Security is as much psychological as physical. Have we not seen just that in our derelict inner cities: the poorest, often ethnic minorities, feeling deprived not only of economic opportunities but also of protection. Those who live on the margins of society become hostile to the system which they feel has rejected them.

The parallels in international terms are becoming very clear. What is developing in the northern hemisphere is a zone of economic well-being which, within a measurable time, will stretch from California eastwards through Europe to the borders of the Soviet Union. In time, one hopes, it will also embrace the USSR, though Soviet problems are on such a scale as to defy early rehabilitation. The same zone will also be governing itself on more or less solid democratic principles.

Within that zone will live pockets of peoples excluded from these benefits. They are likely to be the minorities which have either become voluntarily estranged or been deliberately marginalised because their loyalties are suspected of lying elsewhere. In one case they will need protection; in the other, the world around them is in need of it.

It is on this kind of protection that this book is intended to focus. The fundamental mechanism for ensuring our future security is seen as largely political, directed at two goals: the prevention of conflict by dealing with the conditions which nourish it; and the building of institutions capable of delivering real protection in the hour of need.

What we have witnessed in the 1989 Revolution is a reassertion of the principle of human rights. The spectacle of people rising, without violence or even the means of violence, against their oppressors to demand their rights is awesome enough. Yet the process of forcing the retreat of an unjust system, of pressing until it is replaced with one respecting the dignity of the individual, has brought us into another dimension. What we have witnessed is not just a revolution of the oppressed, but a massive forward movement in man's quest for decency.

That quest for decency, the desire to live in a just society, is the essential fundament on which to build the rule of law between states. It provides the common thread as well as the impulse for joint action and submission to joint institutions. It is also the perfect answer to the ideological vacuum left between the high-flown but empty ideals of Marxism and the equally materialist non-ideology of capitalism.

Security in the eastern European sense must look for its physical expression not to armies but to co-operative policing. For that it will need progressively to develop the right institutions, capable eventually of providing effective guarantees of security. They will not be difficult to devise, nor exacting in the surrenders they demand. The material condition is that all countries should belong to them.

For that, it is crucial to maintain the vision of the world which the bearers of the 1989 Revolution carried with them. So long as they continue to believe in decency, justice and human rights for themselves and their fellow men, so long will it be possible also to speak of a world living in peace and security.

3

NATO—A Shield for All Seasons

'Today, our Alliance begins a major transformation. Working with all the countries of Europe, we are determined to create enduring peace on this continent.'

NATO's London declaration, 6 July 1990

What it is

The Organisation we have known since the North Atlantic Treaty was signed in 1949 is rightly seen as the tangible evidence of the West's determination to defend itself, even to the last. Its 16 members have committed to it at least as much politically as in terms of men and engines of war. Above all, the fact that for 40 years the United States has kept its troops in the forward trenches, rather than as just-in-time reinforcements in the battle to preserve European stability, has been one of the greatest acts of international statesmanship.

NATO's political organs, principally the Atlantic Council, provide a secure roof as well as rigid political control of the military structure. This structure is completely integrated at the three highest levels of command. The process known as ministerial guidance provides the military, political and economic framework for NATO's defence planning. Once assessed by the military authorities in relation to the defence capabilities of both sides, it becomes the basis for the force planning process (FPP), a quite sophisticated mechanism for co-ordinating the defence efforts of participating countries. Each minister of defence eventually agrees to a set of goals, integrated one with another, which his country will endeavour to achieve.

Forces assigned to NATO are integrated to an extent never before seen in peacetime. Its integrated command structure directs a large number of joint operations and services. These include the protective shield of radar installations along the whole eastern front from Norway to Turkey which, together with the airborne AWACS E-3A component, assures NATO's early warning system. For its tele-communications it has established the NATO Communications and Information Systems Agency (NACISA). It also operates a network of facilities for tactical aircraft throughout its forward area, as well as a 10,000-km oil pipeline and storage system.

NATO's Maintenance and Supply Agency (NAMSCO) provides it with the whole array of workshop and engineering services for the maintenance of common weapons systems. Although common procurement policies have been slow to develop, there are several good examples of agreed common projects. The Independent European Programme Group (IEPG) in particular has developed joint production projects and a number of co-operative technology projects based on co-ordination of its members' research efforts.

At operational level, NATO has already succeeded in putting multinational forces in the field. There are three naval forces—in the Atlantic, the Channel and the Mediterranean—composed of ships from various countries. Eight national infantry batallions make up the Allied Command Europe Mobile Force (AMF), whilst the AWACS E-3A component operates 18 aircraft with fully integrated crews from 11 countries. These are examples of low-level integration on regular active operations which are functioning smoothly under a multinational command.

Overall, NATO has achieved a decisive superiority measured against the Warsaw Pact. However, this relies heavily on an advantage in nuclear capability outweighing a serious imbalance in conventional forces. Before German unification, NATO's total armed forces numbered some 3 million men as against the Warsaw Pact's 4 million. More serious disparities existed in the number of tanks, artillery and aircraft. The overall NATO strength, with its implied reliance on early nuclear defence, provoked a major effort to equalise force levels. Three Treaties, for Conventional Forces in Europe (CFE), Intermediate Nuclear Forces (INF) and Strategic Arms Reduction (START), have procured considerable and unequal reductions. They are expected progressively to result in a negotiated balance of forces at quite dramatically lower levels.

What it is not

Whilst honouring NATO's achievements, we should also be aware of what NATO is not. For instance, by no means all the forces of NATO members stationed on the European mainland are committed to it. In particular, the majority of British troops are there under an agreement with Western European Union (WEU), the instrument evolved from the Brussels Treaty to allow, and provide safeguards for, West German rearmament. A condition, negotiated closely with the French and other WEU members, was the stationing of four British divisions and a tactical air force in West Germany. Such commitments would not be affected automatically by changes within NATO.

France does not participate in the Integrated Command Structure. Its forces are therefore wholly autonomous and may, or may not, be committed to NATO in an emergency. Spain also does not commit forces to the Integrated Structure but does participate in the FPP. Iceland has no forces to commit. Greece, Denmark and Norway openly dissent from NATO's nuclear doctrines, at least in peacetime. France takes a wholly independent nuclear stance, as on most other defence matters. On the whole, NATO's ability to influence national plans and actions is slight, even when they accept agreed FPP goals.

NATO is also far from homogeneous. Without vigorous US leadership, it is doubtful how many of the vital operational decisions could have been agreed by Europeans among whom the habit of yielding to the majority has had to develop concurrently. For anyone who wondered why the initiatives had to come from the US side, it was necessary to cast an eye only at the footnotes, caveats and qualifications that were put forward by the smaller members of the alliance. Left to their own devices, the prospects of ever reaching practical decisions would have been much diminished.

Nor were those decisions then necessarily adhered to, especially when defence budgets came under pressure. In 1979 NATO members entered into a commitment to increase defence spending by 3 per cent a year in real terms. Most governments had quietly abandoned this target during the early 1980s, perhaps in a fine anticipation of Mr Gorbachev's arrival. Moves to standardise defence procurement have also usually been thwarted. Development of battle tanks in particular is still regarded as a symbol of national virility.

Now, for the first time since its foundation, NATO genuinely has options. It can make real choices, and it has real and exciting opportunities. Driven by German unification, there are demands for fast decisions, as well as for the right structures within which to make them.

As against that, its very success has called into question its future. As the threat diminishes, people ask why it is necessary to maintain so powerful and expensive an apparatus. Will it not serve to keep the Cold War alive? And could we not put the huge potential savings in military budgets to uses which will actively advance and preserve the new peace? Is not the 'peace dividend' there to be collected, in the interest of our own societies or to shore up the new democracies in eastern Europe?

The riposte to this will clearly depend in the first instance on how much of a threat the Soviet Union could still constitute. Without a doubt, it remains the most powerful force on the European mainland. Its nuclear arsenal, even after removing some of the overkill, is still fearsome. It continues to produce arms at a rapid rate: four tanks a day, 100 tactical air-to-surface missiles a week. There is no let-up in efforts to improve its technological capacity.

Force reductions

Yet CIA estimates are that Soviet defence spending has already fallen by 1.5 per cent; according to the Soviets themselves it was due to be 7 per cent less in 1990 and to fall by a further 10 per cent in 1991. Withdrawals from eastern Europe under the unilateral cuts announced by Mr Gorbachev in his 1989 speech to the UN have already begun; evacuation from Hungary is to be complete by mid–1991. The 380,000 Soviet troops in eastern Germany will be reduced to 275,000 men under the first CFE agreement, then to 195,000, and withdrawn completely by 1994. This will eliminate some of the highly mobile divisions stationed near the old west German border.

The CFE negotiations themselves imply contractual force reductions within NATO. In parallel, however, each NATO member is carrying out its own options review. The British Army of the Rhine (BAOR) will be substantially reduced from its strength of 53,400 men; so will the RAF's Tornado squadrons in Germany. Units moved to the Gulf are unlikely to be returned. The ultimate size of the combined armed forces of the new Germany will not now exceed 370,000 men. Meanwhile the defence budget has been cut by 3 per cent.

Though reluctant to carry out a far-reaching defence review, France is reducing the strength of its forces by 35,000 over the next four years. Substantial cuts, between 15,000 and 20,000 men a year, have already been made in the Italian forces. Much the same applies to Greece and the Netherlands, whilst Belgium also is bringing back some of its forces from Germany. Canada has cancelled substantial orders for nuclear submarines and aircraft, even in advance of its detailed defence review. Denmark, Norway and Turkey are the only members not to announce cuts in 1990.

The same is happening in the USA. There is a continuous stream of defence proposals from all quarters. The result is likely to be a reduction in total forces of 25 per cent over five years. That could mean the disbanding of six out of 18 active-duty army divisions, 11 out of 36 tactical fighter wings, and the scrapping of 110 out of 600 ships. US Forces in Europe might be cut to below 50,000, especially if the Soviet Union carries out its commitment to withdraw all its forces on foreign territory by the year 2000 at the latest.

The justification for these reductions is the new emphasis on light and mobile forces to replace heavy armoured concentrations. The NATO heads of government as a whole have declared that the new allied military strategy will move towards a reduced forward presence and modifications of 'flexible response' to reflect reduced reliance on nuclear weapons. The strategy is likely to set the seal on measures which individual members are already implementing.

These moves present two dangers in the context of the CFE negotiations. One is the establishment of a link between the numbers of US and Soviet troops stationed in Europe. The real aim must surely be to hold the USSR to its pledge for the total removal of Soviet troops from any area outside its own borders, whilst keeping a significant US presence on the European mainland. The second risk is that unilateral scaling down by NATO members will leave nothing in the locker for future CFE negotiations. With greater co-ordination between them, it would be possible to arrive at a more credible negotiating stance as well as a more effective residual force, despite the cuts.

A political NATO

The loss of a clear target and differing perceptions of the residual threat are likely to impose internal strains within the alliance. Even if there is agreement on overall objectives, voters and taxpayers will increasingly question the need for old-style defence budgets. Political leaders will be under pressure to keep expenditures in line with public perceptions.

It follows that there will be little need for a conscious shift towards giving NATO a more political role: both internally and externally, it will in any event face some of its toughest tests in the political arena.

The concept of extra-military functions for NATO is by no means new. Already in 1959, on NATO's tenth anniversary, the Atlantic Congress brought together leaders from all fields of civilian endeavour to search for wider expressions of the role and meaning of the alliance. Many sound recommendations emerged on co-operation between the members and on their responsibilities towards the outside world. Yet, strangely, those that found favour—such as the full membership of Canada and the USA within the Organisation for Economic Co-operation and Development (OECD)—were implemented within organisations other than NATO.

Perhaps this illustrates both the value and the limitations of NATO. On the one hand it is an indispensable instrument of western solidarity. It remains the only body grouping western Europe and the North American democracies. Within it, procedures have been developed for consultations covering all fields of common interest in addition to defence. Since 1985, and the progressive evidence of Mr Gorbachev's intentions, that process has been intensified. NATO summits have become annual; meetings of foreign ministers, in principle biannual, have in practice been much more frequent.

On the other hand, the main impact of this process has been to show that the political masters are firmly in control of the military apparatus. Any consensus achieved on extraneous subjects has invariably served to pollinate other bodies. Thus the 1989 NATO summit declaration on German unification immediately became transmuted into an EC summit declaration, with the added dimension of a Germany anchored in a more fully integrated Community.

Other NATO declarations addressed to the outside world seem to suffer a similar fate. Calls for political, economic and cultural support for the East find the Group of Seven as the forum for their real discussion. When a declaration touches on the world's economic problems, it is careful to stress that member countries will seek to pursue such matters within the appropriate multilateral forum and in close co-operation with other countries.

In short, what is material politically is the ability of the leaders of the West's most active countries to concert their ideas within NATO's consultation processes. That endows NATO with political significance, but it stops well short of lending the organisation itself a political capability.

This is another way of saying that what counts politically is not the North Atlantic Treaty Organisation but rather the North Atlantic Alliance. Whilst NATO is its military manifestation, the political substance resides in the alliance itself. And it is precisely because the military side has been so effective that it dominates, and will continue to overshadow, the alliance which gave birth to it.

We must then ask the question whether the alliance itself could become an effective political organism. Clearly its credibility as such would depend on more than ad hoc consultations among western leaders. It would require three things—a visibly distinctive role, an organisation, and political legitimacy.

The last of these has long been recognised as the missing ingredient. Although the principals in the NATO process are elected members of the constituent governments, their accountability is to their national parliaments. This is unsatisfactory for two reasons: remote decisions, particularly those dealing with security, can never be fully probed; and there is no opportunity for the parliamentarians to participate fully in the processes which they are called upon to scrutinise.

Already in 1956 an attempt was made to bridge this gap. The NATO Parliamentarians' Conference was created to give delegations from national parliaments the opportunity to be briefed and together debate matters of NATO policy and practice. But it was far from being the democratic watchdog which matters of such moment, and commitments of such size, demand. Its conversion into the North Atlantic Assembly gave it greater standing and the ability to question the NATO Council. But it remains a far cry from the kind of parliamentary body needed to generate political momentum. Without this, there is unlikely to be the impetus towards a free-standing political organisation with its own secretariat and other attributes of independence.

Could the alliance then become one of those concentric or overlapping circles which appear to be the future pattern for political and economic advance in Europe? The first answer must, of course, be that it already is one. Because heads of state and foreign ministers are ubiquitous, the alliance is a well-integrated part of the western consultative process. However, for precisely that reason the second answer must be that there is no adequately distinctive function for the alliance—other than its consideration of defence matters. Its main attribute outside that is the cohesion it has brought to western political councils. Whilst it is impossible to exaggerate that achievement, it is an attitudinal rather than institutional one.

Internally within the West, therefore, the alliance is a co-ordinator of defence policy, with all the ramifications which that embraces. Because of its selective membership, which excludes neutral but not unimportant countries, its role is incomplete. Its political influence, whilst considerable, will therefore always be to infuse its policies and decisions into other fora with more internal cohesion as well as their own specific competences.

The same is true of the alliance's external relations. Its military character derives not only from the fact that it manifests itself through NATO. It is predestined to be cast as the West's defence presence simply through the nature of its membership.

From this it follows that neither NATO nor the alliance itself is likely ever to be seen in a primarily political light. It may in future—indeed it will inevitably—play a much more visibly political role; but its remit will remain primarily as the guardian of the West's defences.

A clear medium-term role for NATO

That is clearly a far from negative conclusion. Matters of enormous moment will continue to need to be negotiated and resolved in the defence field. The CFE talks in Vienna must be safely piloted through successive phases. Much hard bargaining remains over nuclear missile systems, and even over stockpiles of chemical and other weapons already outlawed by formal agreement. Only practitioners know what can be negotiated away in safety, what capabilities it is necessary to preserve. Only specialists can work out how to render harmless the most lethal arsenals ever devised.

Until all this has been resolved, and adequate control and verification systems are in place, there is clearly a vital ongoing role for NATO. Politically, realistic negotiations can take place only between the possessors of such weapons. Non-NATO members can make no contribution, other than to assist the process of confidence building in other fora.

A further clear-cut function for NATO will lie in the design of a future pan-European security system. It is one thing to take the political decision to create such a system, quite another to ensure that it is established in a workable fashion. The planning and command structures of such a body, though not as far-reaching, are likely to draw heavily on what has been tested and tried within NATO. The benefit of passing on that knowledge will undoubtedly be timely.

In allowing outsiders to examine its own structures, NATO will itself assist the process of confidence building. In a seemingly para-doxical way, therefore, NATO can also help to allay the suspicions of former adversaries and of the now psychologically non-aligned countries of central and eastern Europe.

A further argument for the retention of NATO for the duration of the process of political change in Europe is that the systems which secured stability and prevented war during the ugly years can still provide that reassurance until the process is complete.

Clearly there are many more reasons why the experience and capabilities within NATO can serve the cause of peaceful transition and reconstruction. One has to think only of the considerable special-ist knowledge its members possess in fields like anti-terrorist, crowd control and interception techniques. All of these will be highly relevant to the mutual security systems to be devised, and greatly more so than combat techniques.

There is thus likely to be a clear role for NATO during the transi-tional period, and as a constructive part of that transition.

That role can be summarised as five basic tasks—(1) to continue adequately to guarantee the security of its members; (2) to contribute to the preservation of stability in central and eastern Europe; (3) to retain a strong US involvement in Europe, whilst encouraging a more cohesive European support; (4) to make a decisive technical contribu-tion to the creation of a pan-European security system, capable of dealing with local conflicts; and (5) to be a valid and effective inter-locutor for both the USA and USSR, and an instrument for building trust rather than dissension.

NATO's western flank

The United States has been present in Europe continuously for half a century. That commitment and its costs are moving dramatically into the centre of the US domestic agenda. NATO's immediate battle ground now lies on its highly exposed western flank, in Washington.

For years the world has been aware of the mounting US budget deficit. The message has been heard that the US is now the world's largest debtor, eclipsing the debt of all the third world taken together. So long as the Japanese were willing to finance that, we all somehow felt that we could live with it.

Now that the deficit appears to have gone out of control, we sud-denly have to wake up. Even before the Gulf conflict began a total deficit of US$254 billion was budgeted for 1991. That would have compared with a 1991 ceiling of US$64 billion under the unamended Gramm–Rudman deficit-reduction legislation. The US Administration finds itself caught between automatic spending cuts and tax increases. Neither alternative is palatable, and the former could lead to a deepening recession. But so—for certain hitherto favoured areas––could a drastic peace dividend.

The signs of recession are already clear: collapse of the New England construction industry, plummeting sales of the Michigan automobile industry, defence establishment lay-offs in California and elsewhere. Even if some others—Ohio, Wisconsin, Nevada—are still prospering, these are unmistakable pointers. Some estimates are predicting the loss of one million jobs over the coming five years.

In part the problem is structural. Imports and exports are greatly out of balance. Large oil imports, a new feature of more recent years, are inconsistent with the domestic price of gasoline. That and tax increases are 'holy cows', to be disturbed only at one's peril. Other problems are man-made, such as banking deregulation and the nationwide collapse of savings-and-loan institutions. Bailing them out will constitute some US$60 billion of the 1991 deficit alone. As elsewhere, social problems are making ever-greater claims on budgets.

Military expenditures have, not unnaturally, formed a substantial part of the budget, even though the trend has been steadily downwards. As a percentage of gross national product they have fallen from 7 per cent to 5 per cent since 1985. Their share of total government spending has also shown a sustained decline, from a historic high in 1950 to something approaching 20 per cent today. The Bush Administration's current estimates project further declines up to 1995 in both ratios. The 1991 defence budget has already been cut by 3 per cent in real terms, to a total of US$288 billion. Another source, the analyst William Kaufmann, has demonstrated that defence spending could be reduced from that figure to US$160 billion a year by the end of the decade.

Proposals drawn up by the Pentagon, as well as House and Senate bills, envisage a radical restructuring of the US army. They foresee a highly mobile contingency force, based mainly in the US but capable of rapid deployment elsewhere. The European theatre would no longer be its central objective. That could bring a reduction in forces from 2.1 million to 1.6 million by 1995, including transfer to the Gulf of 50,000 men based in Germany.

US expenditure in connection with its presence in Europe has been a massive $150 billion a year. Ironically, that approximates to the size of the current underlying budget deficit. For psychological reasons as well as hard reality, the focus will alight on stationed forces in Europe. Withdrawing 50,000 US servicemen, even if for duties elsewhere, will reduce expenditure in Europe by close on US$5 billion a year.

Both the Pentagon's New Global Strategy and the House of Representatives envisage bringing home most of the 450,000 US troops more or less permanently stationed abroad before the Gulf build-up. That might leave no more than 25,000-50,000 US servicemen in Europe. A Washington research group, the Defense Budget Project, is said to have calculated that the withdrawal of 100,000 troops would liberate another 100,000 support personnel and save an almost irresistible US$30 billion.

The implications are substantial. No US President can afford not to act on the spiralling budget deficit. No President can allow US troops to be stationed in Europe without means of adequate protection. Somewhere between these two imperatives a residual strength must be found which is affordable, able to defend itself until reinforced from the USA, and shielded by the nuclear umbrella.

Such a specification will lead to some hard bargaining with US allies. All of them are concerned to see the US commitment to Europe confirmed with a visible and effective military presence. Opinions may be divided over the optimum size and the physical location of US forces, but the principle is clearly acknowledged. Greater divisions exist over the nuclear aspect, in particular the need for continued modernisation and up-dating of the hardware.

Much will turn on collective decisions on these matters taken by the united Germany. Given the present sentiment, both modernisation and nuclear silos on German soil will be deeply unpopular. With France not participating in NATO's command structure and unwilling to receive nuclear arms, where could they then be stationed? Whether or not nuclear arms or their carriers are to be located on German soil has to be a German decision, though arrived at in consultation with her allies. How would the UK and others react if they had to play host to systems rejected by Germany?

Much more might well be read into such a decision. Could a Germany without nuclear weapons lead to the 'nuclear-free zone' once held out by the USSR as a condition for unification? Could that in turn lead to neutralising Germany and—despite Soviet acquiescence to continued membership—loosening of its bonds with NATO? Above all, could it retain US confidence that its remaining forces would continue to be adequately protected?

The United States' peace dividend

Substantial cuts in defence spending would, of course, produce dislocations in the US economy. These could even be severe in some states which, like California, rely heavily on the defence industry. Estimates by SRI International, a part of Stanford Research Institute, show, however, that these are likely to be relatively short-term. A fall of 2 per cent a year in real terms over five years would mean reduced economic growth—with lower inflation—until the end of year six. But growth thereafter would be faster than if spending had continued at today's levels. The federal budget deficit might also shrink to US$48 billion.

The effects of a 5 per cent annual reduction, again in real terms, would be more dramatic. Apart from putting the federal budget into surplus, they would yield even stronger economic growth after an interim downturn and, above all, sharply declining interest rates. Already from year three onwards, these would work rapidly through the economy, in particular stimulating investment and the construction industry.

Defence-related industries would release large numbers of scientists, engineers and technicians. They currently employ some 17 per cent of US engineers, 5 per cent of the scientists and over 7 per cent of computer specialists. They also account for 20 per cent of employment in the manufacture of radio and TV equipment, scientific instruments, industrial vehicles and aircraft.

The effect on these, and the more obvious defence equipment manufacturers, would be severe, with extensive dislocations of their labour and professionals. The corollary of defence spending cuts would therefore be some increase in social costs, but with the prospect of a relatively early adjustment taking place. Unemployment at the end of the six-year period is projected at 4.7 per cent, as against a no-change 5.2 per cent.

Such calculations are substantiated by research done by Cambridge University based econometrists, which indicates that the same is likely to be true of the UK. A cumulative cut of 50 per cent by the end of the decade is estimated to produce a substantial increase in employment and gross domestic product.

It is clear that the peace dividend has substantial attractions both for people and—provided that the political penalties of adjustment prove containable—for the US Administration. Indeed, the search will be on for the cross-over point at which those penalties risk being outweighed by disappointed public expectations. One simple determinant is likely to be the insistent daily reminders of social and neighbourhood problems, poverty, homelessness and drug abuse, whilst the need to save the free world from tyranny recedes further and further from the headlines. Significantly, two-thirds of Americans polled are looking to the peace dividend not with trepidation for their jobs but as a medicament to heal their social ills.

Preserving cohesion

Other perceptions may also undermine the feeling of United States' solidarity with Europe. The European Community is becoming a superpower in its own right. In trade matters it already acts as a single bloc. There have been trade skirmishes where interests collided, and more abiding disagreements over farm subsidies and export rebates. Will US opinion sustain its support for Atlantic unity when it sees the EC becoming an economic competitor second only to Japan?

Both public and officials are quick to extrapolate events into trends. The more independent stance taken recently by Germany and Japan has quickly been translated into the 'go-your-own-way era' in which the US is losing its traditional position as steersman of the West. The reality of the new situation is to be found more in the widening field of trade-offs necessary to strike bargains and achieve common positions on issues of concern to the US. The go-ahead for German lending to an as yet unreconstructed Soviet economy is traded for progress on agricultural export subsidies within the GATT negotiations—but with Germany also conceding a less costly approach for cleaning up the US environment. Capital for reconstructing eastern Europe, but not the Soviet Union, is the price for Japan's desire to assist a still undemocratic China.

But there are sterner tests to come. Any conceivable development of NATO will demand greater flexibility. Both its objectives and its horizons will no longer be fixed. For five decades we have lived with certainties: first that Hitler must be defeated and a just peace assured; then, that the Soviet menace must be resisted at all costs. Can we now adjust to the uncertainty of a creative political process? Can minor political ambitions, for long subordinated to the overall goal, be kept in check without rocking the consensus?

The need for cohesion and rapid decision making will remain and, if anything, increase. Decisions will, by definition, have to be taken in response to unpredictable events. Although the new challenges to peace are likely to be relatively minor, they may arise anywhere within the area of instability that is eastern Europe. The lack of a specific focus will be a severe test for our will to maintain a political commitment to the alliance.

Without a focus, without a predictable hypothesis of where to target forces, it will be impossible to design a security system along classic lines. Moving towards a new 'structure' may therefore be an illusion. Can the West maintain the will to deal purposefully with an evolving situation, or will flexibility and uncertainty undermine its cohesion?

A contrary danger is that we try to compensate for the uncertainty by encasing ourselves in hastily conceived structures and institutions. The temptation is real, as a man-made counter to the challenge of finding oneself at the mercy of events. The only alternatives are strong leadership and a belief in a firm political direction. Otherwise our need for order will block more intelligent and far-seeing responses as the situation evolves.

There are other temptations that could deflect us, particularly in our perception of new threats. To the East, the military capacity of the Soviet Union is still awesome and could yet be unleashed by accident, or through desperation if the colossus were to disintegrate. The West will have a clear task to protect all of us—including the people of the USSR—against that ever happening. It is not difficult to detect other threats developing further South: population issues, famine, the rape of the world's environment, drugs, religious fundamentalism. They are undoubtedly real, but they may also become excuses for keeping in place defensive structures for no better reason than to retain our cohesion. Iraq notwithstanding, the search for new enemies should be left to Don Quixote. Out-of-area actions will be of deep concern for the alliance; but any NATO function is likely to be restricted to co-ordination of peace-keeping forces placed under some different command.

The European pillar

A crucial inducement for the US to remain in Europe will be greater burden-sharing. If the US Administration is to hold the line on its commitment, it needs a clear signal that its European allies are prepared to shoulder a fair share of the overall cost of a radically overhauled defence effort. The smaller the US forces, the greater the need to keep a nuclear deterrent for their protection. Despite maintaining their own independent nuclear capacity, the United Kingdom and

France, along with other Europeans, will have to shoulder a larger proportion of the common defence than they do at present.

With everyone already looking to spend the peace dividend, that may not be welcome news. Nor will it be easy to agree on what may well be an unequal adjustment; the UK, for instance, spends 50 per cent more on defence as a proportion of its gross domestic product than did West Germany alone. It will be even less attractive to those who believe that NATO has done its defence job and see its future role in pressing disarmament and monitoring arms controls. To them, the less force and efficiency it possesses, the better qualified it will be to form the nucleus of a new security system threatening nobody.

This is an updated version of the tug-of-war between hawks and doves which has been the perennial feature of the NATO alliance. But so far from being an inherent weakness, this tension has always been part of its strength. It has simply served to confuse the enemy. In the new situation, conflicting signals may present more of a danger. But with much hard bargaining still to be done, such signals can project the right assurances that a stoutly defended position is never an immutable roadblock; it merely needs patience and the right offer to lead to agreement.

Yet with all that, the choice is simple. If we want the US to stay in Europe, there is a price to pay. Predictably, the price of letting the Atlantic alliance drift apart would be incalculably higher. No one pretends that a presence in Europe is not also in the interest of the US. What counts is that that presence should be an earnest of the US commitment to the common destiny, not merely to its own.

The price has to be counted not just in the old terms of stationing costs and offsets. The cost of technology to maintain and update an effective capability is steadily becoming greater. Technology has long since lost its protection, even in the initial years until others arrived at the same point. Today it can no longer be kept secret. In consequence, the need to counter and surpass has become ever more pressing, and the escalations in time and costs ever higher.

We are at the point where only superpowers have the resources to keep up. The USSR—a superpower militarily, in economic terms a developing country—has already begun to flag. Only the USA and the nascent superpower of a united European Community can continue to shoulder such responsibilities.

On top of these economic considerations are the purely practical. If NATO has at least a medium-term role, in whatever form, it must retain not only its political cohesion but also an efficient command structure. It must have the capacity to devise a swift response, and then to implement it. What can be the realistic prospects of that unless the Europeans are able to get their own act together? In the early years of the alliance a favourite phrase was 'the giant and the pygmies'. Now, at least in political and economic terms, those pygmies have reached the age of consent.

Clearly the EC is destined to play a preponderant role. It is already leading the western effort of economic assistance to the new eastern democracies. It should also be the body most closely concerned with the political restructuring of Europe. In parallel with pressing bilateral affairs, the US has begun to use it for consultations. US leaders now make two stops in Brussels: at NATO HQ and at the EC Commission.

Within the EC, political, economic and monetary union are on the agenda. Is it possible to develop either its internal or its external status without a security dimension? The concept is by no means new. One of the earliest proposals for European union was the European Defence Community, unsuccessfully broached in 1954. More recently, the 1986 Single European Act made reference to security in the chapter on co-operation in the sphere of foreign policy. Yet that still respected the fact that, alone among the twelve, the Republic of Ireland is neutral and therefore not a member of NATO.

Unique is also the position which France occupies within NATO. Since 1966 France has not taken part in NATO's Defence Planning Committee or the Military Committee, nor has it committed any forces to NATO command. Yet it accepts the obligations of the Treaty for joint defence, and other allies retain their obligation for the defence of France. It also uniquely provides NATO with a counter-attack force, designed to re-establish the cohesion of forward defence in case of need. It continues to participate in all NATO activities outside the military, and particularly in political consultation. Its famed domestic 'consensus' in defence matters rests on nuclear deterrence, autonomy of decision in matters of peace and war, and self-reliance in military equipment.

The issue of neutrality may well become more relevant in the future. Austria, whose neutrality is implied by the Staatsvertrag, has already applied for EC membership. If the remaining countries of the European Free Trade Area were to exercise that option, this would add two further neutrals, Sweden and Switzerland. One-quarter of an enlarged membership would then prefer neutrality. Obviously, prospects for a common EC defence strategy would be reduced. The problem could be compounded by eventual membership of the new eastern democracies.

Where does that leave a potential EC 'security dimension'? Much will depend on the extent to which the present political co-operation becomes converted into a real political union. Remote as it may seem, especially in the light of current disagreements in the UK over the forms of the EC's political and economic integration, the wheels are turning almost inexorably in that direction. Driven by German unification, and Germany's own desire to ensure that it is accompanied by making the links between EC partners truly indissoluble, it has acquired considerable momentum.

Political union should then lead directly to a common foreign policy. And it is clear that security is an indispensable dimension of foreign policy. Already in the Single European Act, EC members pledged themselves to endeavour to adopt common positions in international institutions and consultations, and to avoid all acts which might impair their effectiveness as a cohesive force in such bodies. That has already had implications for both NATO and WEU. Fuller political union would make it mandatory for EC members to act as a group, and its institutions would ensure this in practice.

Thus the security interests of the EC would become served within a common foreign policy and a common approach to their partners. But that would not immediately involve them in the business of defence and military decision making, responsibility for which would still lie outside the EC itself. What then is to be the bridge between the EC and the European pillar of NATO?

In all but name and formal recognition as such, this already exists in Western European Union (WEU). It antedates the EC and received its principal impetus from the need to control the rearming of West Germany. It already incorporates the majority of the EC's NATO members, including France, which plays a full and virtually unconditional role within it. Of course, its purpose and procedures differ markedly from NATO. Some of its organs, such as the Standing Armaments Committee, employ similar approaches and would blend well into any more formal association with NATO.

An additional advantage is that WEU has its own parliamentary Assembly, which could link easily with the European Parliament and its relevant committees. WEU would therefore mesh both politically and democratically with the EC, yet without causing distress to those EC members not involved. As it happens, interest in WEU has recently revived and its prestige has been enhanced, particularly through its co-ordinating role for the European naval force sent to the Gulf. Although this is the closest it has come to an operational function, it could offer a realistic foundation on which to build the executive arm of an EC security policy, as well as the European pillar of NATO.

The German dimension

Even though the major hurdle of Soviet agreement to the new Germany's membership of NATO has been swiftly overcome, it is impossible to avoid addressing the issue of Germany's military and diplomatic status. It is—and clearly can now remain—an indispensable part of NATO. To the extent that the five new *Länder* of the former German Democratic Republic have acceded to it, its membership also remains constitutionally unaffected. Politically, there is no doubt that this is the wish of the German people themselves, of its allies, and even of a good section of opinion among its neighbours to the East.

Yet the sheer size and economic importance of the new Germany raise a number of questions. The first is a matter of balance. The sole way to maintain the balance of forces needed to inhibit domination by any single continental power is to keep the US in Europe. Only the US has the size and ability to act as a counterweight—whether defensively to the USSR or, more psychologically, to tomorrow's Germany.

Keeping the US in Europe has been taken as synonymous with retaining US troops, principally in Germany. That is the hostage view, which holds that they must be there as a trigger to bring the whole of the US to their defence. It suffers from a fatal flaw: without the conviction that the USA's security is linked to that of Europe, the hostages are likely to be withdrawn. In the new Europe, the common interest demands that the US believes itself to have a vital role as arbiter, moderator and counterpoise.

It also demands a strong link between Germany and the US. How could this be affected if German public opinion were to reject the stationing of US—or any other—forces, and their nuclear weapons, on its soil? There are visible dangers ahead, as well as possibly invisible ones. Could the agreement between Mr Gorbachev and Chancellor Kohl on Germany's continued membership of NATO have been based on wider understandings, whose effects are yet to emerge? What is clear already is that the Stavropol agreement contains a pledge to keep nuclear weapons out of eastern Germany. Is it feasible for Germany to have them on one part of its territory and not on another?

A more independent German policy may also serve to estrange the US. Mr Kohl's lack of contact with Washington on that occasion should not be a portent. The US is beginning to note with dismay that its permission is no longer sought on an increasing list of matters with which Germany and Europe have begun to deal independently. Frequent direct contacts with the USSR over its troops in eastern Germany may increase these sensitivities further.

Provoked by Iraq, the issue of German troops being dedicated solely to defence within the NATO area has moved onto the agenda. On the one hand, such a restrictive status may be difficult to reconcile with Germany's new sovereignty after the official ending of four-power control. On the other, the out-of-area prohibition prevents German forces being attached even to a UN peace-keeping mission.

All these matters will need to be carefully tended, lest at some stage they prejudice NATO's cohesion and capacity to carry out its proper role. The key to some of these problems may well lie in more integration of forces and the allocation of special roles to individual members of NATO. In fact, the new concept of more mobile and versatile defence offers such possibilities by way of role specialisation. They could well become a functional answer to pre-empt some of the potential strains within the alliance.

'Love your neighbour, but keep your fence up'

All such considerations lead inexorably to certain conclusions about the role of NATO in the medium term:

- So long as the process of transition in Europe is neither clear nor complete, NATO will be needed as an alliance to concert policy; as an instrument for negotiations on present, future and interim security; and as a shield to ensure that the process of transition is peacefully carried through.
- Although judicious force and capability reductions are desirable both in themselves and as negotiating factors, the time for dismantling the existing military structure is certainly not yet.
- NATO has always had a political dimension and demanded a political commitment from its members. This needs now to be sensibly reinforced, towards the outside world as well as to maintain and improve its internal command structure.

- A western consensus on eastern Europe, west European integration and partnership for global stability must be maintained.
- A continuing US presence in Europe is a vital part of that consensus; but this can be assured only if the cost to the US is drastically reduced and greater responsibilities are assumed by the Europeans.
- Germany must remain closely integrated within the Atlantic and European elements of the alliance. The crucial task is, and will remain, to provide both the US and the USSR with reassurances about their own security concerns as they perceive them.
- The bipolar balance of power has disappeared. The only alternative to it is integration.

4

From Confrontation to Peace-keeping

'What were we supposed to do? Should we have used axes and tanks and tried to teach them another lesson in how to live?'

PRESIDENT GORBACHEV, when accused of losing eastern Europe

The world in transition

If it is clear that NATO has an essential role to perform in the short and medium term, it is equally obvious that it will need to undergo certain changes. Its conversion from a tool of Cold War trials of strength and a symbol of unchallengeable might into a convincing servant of peaceful confidence building will be a far-reaching process. Only at some more advanced stage will it become clear whether such radical change can be wrought within NATO itself or whether this will then require an instrument of a different kind and calibre.

The evolution we are witnessing in Europe today has already gone beyond the immediately obvious: the loss of an enemy (as Mr Gorbachev himself pointed out), the virtual disintegration of the Warsaw Pact, the reduction of force levels and the redefining of objectives and targets. In effect, these are only the outward signs of an underlying historical process in which both sides of the European divide have been caught up. Only now that we have seen its first dramatic results can we begin to gauge the force of the historical undertow which is sweeping us into such unfamiliar waters.

We can identify at least four strands to this process. First, the coalescing of communities into larger units—a process we can trace back at least to the middle ages—has jolted the world another step forward. The last major upheaval occurred in the 19th century, when the remaining principalities merged into nation states. Like seismic disturbances, the shock-waves of new nations competing with the old, have rumbled on for nearly two centuries. Following the cataclysmic eruptions of the two world wars, they have finally reached some form of equilibrium.

Now, it seems, we are preparing for the next step. The emergence of the superpowers was surely no accident. Once the *pax britannica* had faded, and with it the concept of a benign protector and fair referee in global affairs, a competitive system was bound to emerge. It did so, but reluctantly. The USA, brought onto the world stage early this century and onto the European stage through the First World War, was hesitant to assume the British mantle. Although it soon became an empire in the Pacific, and knew how to defend its interests in its own hemisphere, a formal global role smacked still of the colonialism from which the US itself was born. The cost of withdrawing from Europe and its concerns, then being forced to come back a second time, was incalculable.

Western Europe, too, has been reluctant to accept the challenge. The countries which were occupied during the Second World War were, not unnaturally, the first to see the need for a different form of governance in Europe. The European Community, in its early restricted form and limited membership, was their first practical attempt. It took fifteen years for the UK and others to join, and a further fifteen for all northern Mediterranean countries to become members. Even now, full economic and political union is still a distant, though at last discernible goal.

The realisation by its members of the EC's destiny to become a superpower has been equally halting. Like Gertrude Stein's *Ugly Dachshund*, the bulldog who saw himself as one of the lap-dogs with whom he grew up, there is an occasional awareness of an untoward attribute: grasping that one is the world's largest consumer of cocoa, being pressed into the western front-line for aid to eastern Europe, finding oneself responsible for dealing with a major part of the greenhouse effect. Yet, aside from the fact that virtually all its members form part of the NATO alliance—and despite both headquarters being in the same city—the concept of the EC as such developing a security policy is only now being faced.

Notwithstanding the reluctance of either of these superpowers, the nascent Soviet Union saw itself threatened, first by its capitalist neighbours to the west, including Germany, then by the whole of the

west including the USA. For the USSR, the alliance was the conclusive symbol of an implacable hostility between two opposing
ideologies. The fact that it was their ideology which taught that
capitalism was incapable of co-existing with communism made not
one jot of difference to their perception.

States which feel themselves threatened develop the raw ambition
to compete with others over whom they seek to gain supremacy.
Those others in turn find themselves challenged to retain their position. Either alone or jointly with others similarly aroused, they need
rapidly to develop their defences and their economic capacity. The
result is a competitive leap-frogging in which any small advantage
tends soon to be cancelled out. It becomes a basically unstable situation in which all participants are forced to accept unwanted burdens.
At best, one player will resign exhausted; at worst, he will forestall
such a defeat by using his expensively accumulated arsenal. The
intermediate state is the stalemate of the Cold War with which we
lived for forty years.

Allied with the trend towards larger and supra-national communities, there has been a change in our perception of sovereignty.
Whatever differences may persist over how such communities should
be administered for the benefit and with the consent of their members,
most of us acknowledge that they have their legitimate place. One
may prefer common action in trade negotiations, another in development aid, yet another in defence. Few will nowadays argue that
nations can preserve their old glory by standing alone; or expect
others to go our way without some pledge of reciprocity from us.

A third trend then is the dissolution of the nation state from within.
As communities of states become larger, and the patriotic claim of the
state to the absolute loyalty of its citizens is challenged, so the
individual becomes free to rediscover his more immediate affiliations.
There is a re-awakening of far older communities and societies, of
ethnic ties and cultures, of languages and linkages between regions
rather than states. Former nations of Celts and Basques, of Serbians
and Azerbaijanis, of Latvians and Lombards, are resuming their identities—and sometimes their old enmities. This cultural separatism
does not automatically imply the political or economic dissolution of
the state or community of which they have formed part. But it will
require considerable respect and ingenuity if stresses are to be
contained.

The fourth underlying trend turns on the advance of technology. To
a significant extent this has been the result of superpower competi-

tion, of the arms race and the needs of expanding economies. It has made some things impossible, such as meeting the bills for ever more costly improvements of weapons and defensive systems—not to mention the grim consequences of actually using them. At the same time, technology has made other things possible: devising adequate means of control and verification, finding peaceful and remunerative uses for defence industries and establishments, allowing countries without traditional raw materials to flourish, helping to avert some of the causes of world poverty and hence of conflict itself.

How to adapt

The lessons to be drawn from these developments are relatively clear. In the first place we need to develop a security system which is no longer competitive but based upon a recognition of the security needs of others living in our space. That means primarily the organisation of security zones within which clear principles prevail and dispositions of forces and installations are open to security partners from other co-operating zones. It follows that a common security arrangement ought to be based not on individual countries with vetoes and different ideas, but on the interaction between the larger communities.

Such an arrangement will have immediate implications for the EC, since it implies as great a challenge to arrive at a common security policy as does the doctrine of the European pillar. The need for such a policy will be inescapable, whether the EC chooses to exercise it through the Western European Union or direct.

But the EC is not the only community to be challenged by this principle. The USSR may find it increasingly difficult to remain as spokesman and plenipotentiary in military matters for all its present republics. Much will depend on its ability to devise a system of governance which will combine an acceptable measure of internal independence with a commensurate degree of authority in external affairs.

Perhaps the most substantial historical consequence to be faced is that newly embraced ethnic allegiances will increasingly impair the ability to mobilise large armies. Whereas in former times the possession of territory and vassals meant the ability to raise regiments, today the opposite is more likely to be true. Loyalty to the nation state is no longer automatic; whilst that to a larger community is neither formed nor likely to develop. The outbreak of hostilities may in future be seen more as the failure of one's own government rather than the iniquity of whoever dares to breach the new peace.

If a future threat to peace is thus more likely to have its roots in ethnic rather than national conflict, there will be important consequences for the composition of forces. Steps are already being taken in the USSR to constitute units free of recruits from republics which may secede from the Union, or where forces may have to be sent to control local unrest. Much the same will apply to troops composing a common security system, one of whose principal functions would certainly become the quelling of such conflicts.

Lastly, the concept of significant and durable technological superiority must be abandoned. Not only its cost but its substance has moved out of reach. Open skies, the collapse of frontiers enclosing knowledge, have meant effectively that we can match what others possess, but we cannot overtake them or gain an advantage for a significant length of time. Hence it is lapses of concentration rather than a sustained research and development effort which are in future likely to put us at a disadvantage.

What is quite certain is that our task now is to take full advantage of these historical processes which have moved in our favour. They have produced a fluidity in world affairs which, like Shakespeare's tide, can lead us on to a unique fortune of opportunities. Seize it we must, unless, as in 1918 and in 1945, we want once again to forfeit the gains we have made.

The new challenges

Yet there are already new challenges to peace. Deposing tyrants, freeing societies, resurrecting human rights are victories for humankind; but they also free ambitions long suppressed. In a newly liberated society it is difficult to distinguish between the voices crying for the right to self-expression and those seeking self-determination. In the first moments, democracy is the password which admits all.

So long as the transition from confrontation to co-operation can be managed peacefully, it is evident that threats to pan-European security and stability will arise from two sources: internal dissent and flashpoints outside Europe. The first of these is typified by minority problems and ethnic violence, of the kind which, for example, the British are familiar with in Northern Ireland, and the embroiling of otherwise friendly states. Examples of the second are also not hard to find: predator countries like Iraq provoking full-scale wars, areas of

perennial fracture like Lebanon and Cambodia, and the lawlessness of
hostage taking.

The first kind will set new tasks for NATO or any successor in the
security field. The second, though out-of-area, will pose new tests for
the Atlantic alliance as well as the members of the new pan-European
security zone. Both will need to be on the security agenda of the
superpowers, including the EC.

Neither can, by definition, be the subject of specific targeting.
There is no historic or likely major enemy, no front to secure, no
pillboxes to be built. Red is no longer the colour of the invader on
manoeuvres. Curiously, we are precisely in the situation enunciated
for France a generation ago by General de Gaulle—of vigilance on all
sides. His strategy of *tous azimuts*, all points of the compass, amounted
to a general alert which took in France's African and Middle Eastern
obligations of the time and therefore covered well what we now call
out-of-area conflicts.

One of the gravest possibilities of internal dissent rests, of course,
within the Soviet Union. The tensions building up between the
Kremlin and the individual republics are plain to see. Some are at
the local level, relieving pent-up hatreds such as those between
Armenians and Azerbaijanis. Others concern direct challenges to
Moscow's rule from smaller and essentially foreign annexations like
the Baltic republics of Estonia, Latvia and Lithuania. But then there
are the gargantuan trials of strength between the centre and such core
territories as the Russian Federation or the Ukraine. Almost all the
Soviet Union's 15 republics have now declared their sovereignty—
not, as initially in Lithuania, independence—and most have
stipulated their military neutrality.

The Kremlin's steely resistance to local autonomy and dismemberment of the Union has already drawn blood. However, if the Soviet
army and security forces were ordered to mount a full-scale
repression, it is hard to see how a charge of aggression could be
avoided. At one time it seemed that the point of no return had been
passed, where armed action to subdue dissident republics was no
longer a valid option. A good indicator will be the extent to which the
decree making it mandatory to disarm 'illegal armed groups'—i.e.
local defence militias—can be enforced.

In addition to natural resistance to seeing the USSR disintegrate,
there remains one external factor which could be used to justify the
use of force to keep the Union together. A preponderant German role,
whether within NATO or alone, could be made a suasion to corral the

recalcitrants together once more. Continuing the process of negotiation in every forum from CFE to CSCE, the willingness to demonstrate flexibility and an understanding of the Soviet leader's need to bring home occasional concessions—of which few have been vouchsafed so far—will be the West's contribution to seeing that this card cannot be played.

Quite clearly, there are no conceivable circumstances in which NATO members or anyone else would aim to intervene in any conflict within the Soviet Union, however grievous it would be to see newly-won freedoms and democracy extinguished. The same should not be true of the other countries of eastern Europe. Military means would still be ruled out—unless there were, within the CSCE or a similar framework, a mechanism for unambiguously requesting such assistance, and answering it with a multinational unit responding to that call. It follows that one of the priorities of negotiations must be to establish that kind of framework as rapidly as possible.

A further imperative is to ensure that the former Warsaw Pact countries are able to make steady progress to emerge from their poverty and social sufferings. That will require a co-operative effort outside the security field, and the transfer of quite massive resources. As has been shown, significant action has already been taken jointly and severally by 24 western donor countries, as well as by the EC which is co-ordinating the programme, by the World Bank group and by the new European Bank for Reconstruction and Development (EBRD). This is an essential part of the confidence-building process, backing up fine words about democracy by helping them to achieve its reality. Yet, whilst the USSR should also be reassured by the removal of poverty and tensions from its borders, it cannot consider itself in the same favoured company unless it too is bidden to the feast.

Local strife, then, will constitute a particular hazard until the means are in place to deal with it uncontroversially and, little by little, to eradicate some of its causes. Measures to maintain security will therefore need to be a mixture of the political, economic and military. One thing, however, is certain; they will require neither offensive nor defensive weapons or forces.

A different aspect of unrest could be prompted by the patent spread of extremists in Europe. The extreme right-wing Le Pen movement has gained much ground in France, worryingly across the social spectrum, and has markedly affected the stance of other parties.

Untypically for Italy, racism has erupted in Florence, Milan, Rome and Turin. Austria's xenophobic Freiheitliche Partei has scored alarming election successes with a neo-nazi platform. There as elsewhere, we see evidence of a rising tide of anti-semitism.

In the UK, racial harassment has been directed particularly at the Asian community, but at Afro-Caribbeans as well. Muslim extremists took to the streets over Salman Rushdie's book, the *Satanic Verses*, and even announced a separatist movement. Perhaps the most perturbing recent development has been the appeal of the neo-nazi Republican Party and its earlier election successes in West Germany. Together with other right-wing groups, their ranks have been swelled not only by the appeal to restless youth but by discontent over the influx of east Europeans.

All this is a timely reminder that Germany, like the USSR, like much of eastern and western Europe and even the United Kingdom, has disaffected minorities, contested borders, diaspora communities, racism and xenophobia. It therefore also has all the vulnerability of any democracy to nationalist emotion. In a democracy such emotions need to find their outlet on the hustings and at the ballot box; one should not be unduly alarmed when they do. It is the clandestine movements and the bully boys that would be the real enemies. The movement of peoples across the face of Europe is bound to cause frictions and dislocations. Nevertheless, the resurgence of crude political responses will require a good deal of vigilance.

An altogether different set of problems may obtain on NATO's flanks, in particular the southern one. Both geographic location and its ethnic composition make Turkey particularly vulnerable. It could easily be drawn into local conflicts spilling over from Armenia or one of the southern Soviet republics. It is sensitive to the fate of the large Turcoman populations in many parts of the USSR; on both ethnic and religious grounds it may present a particular focus for them. It must be assumed that Turkey's longest-standing problem, that with Greece over Cyprus, can continue to be controlled within the alliance; but friction with the Soviet Union would be an altogether more hazardous development.

Problems of a more threatening kind have already made themselves felt on Turkey's borders with Iran, Iraq and Syria. The Kurdish minority, the proximity of Muslim fundamentalism, and a belligerent and expansionist neighbour intent on stalking the Middle East do not augur well for stability on the southern flank. It is here that the NATO alliance's perennial problem of responses to out-of-area conflicts is most likely to be tested.

For both Europe and the USA, the Middle East represents an area of irremediable instability. From Israel and the Palestinian problem to the insecurity of the Gulf and its oilfields, from religious warfare in Lebanon to the zealots of Iran, from Iraqi invaders to Libyan exports of terrorism, it is a minefield of accidents waiting—indeed eager—to happen. What the West has at stake varies from the domestic political issues raised by the vulnerability of Israel, to the economic interests involved in oil flows. The latter are heightened by the zest with which individual countries of both West and East have chosen to supply arms to the potential combatants. Over the past two years, two-thirds of all arms sold to the Third World went to the Middle East, and indiscriminately to all sides. Thus there are good customers to be considered, their mounting debts to be protected, and thousands of advisers and technicians to be safeguarded.

Other flashpoints are becoming more quiescent. Afghanistan, itself at one time a Middle Eastern issue because of the Soviet shadow over the oil veins of the Persian Gulf, has changed from a threat to an embarrassment. It is but the latest example of the instability left behind on old superpower battlegrounds. From Vietnam to Cambodia, from Ethiopia to Nicaragua, conflict persists as those supported by their respective superpower fight on for supremacy. Once, they suffered the withdrawal symptoms on the departure of the colonial or protecting power; now they face a new crisis as the superpowers bury their differences.

As formerly when the British faced the wind of change in Africa and elsewhere, the ballot box has become the favoured exit mechanism. It allows the superpower to depart with a clear conscience, having set in motion the democratic process so long denied by force of arms. There are promising examples, like Nicaragua and Namibia, but their durability remains to be tested. Others have led to renewed fighting and, at worst, a resumption of the vicious spiral of foreign involvement. Some, like Kuwait, have temporarily ceased to exist.

Finding new responses

A coherent western response to such problems has been notoriously difficult to achieve. There are inevitable disagreements on principle, and often over the exigencies of economic interest. Some dislike the use of force, others object to sanctions. Some are hostages to their commercial interest, others to a political lobby. And yet others are unconcerned because they have neither.

During the Iran-Iraq war (1980–1987), NATO experienced the

greatest difficulty in a search for combined action to safeguard its members' shipping in the Persian Gulf. When in the end WEU took on the co-ordination, it had taken the UK, France, Italy and the USA a full eight years from the outbreak of that war to put together their Armilla Patrol. There has been a more purposeful approach within the Atlantic Council during the Gulf campaign, no doubt as a result of the succession of recent political contacts. Nevertheless, there are sound reasons why NATO should not seek a global out-of-area role. In reality, it is much more likely that responses to such crises will always need to be selective and ad hoc.

Yet it is clear that the West has a vital interest in defusing or diminishing such conflicts wherever they may occur. One increasingly compelling reason is the already lengthy list of countries on the threshhold of nuclear capability. There is a real prospect that one or more of these presently 14 countries will be tempted to exercise regional nuclear blackmail. Even more alarmingly, several may already have the ability to target European territory.

In other ways, however, the changed policies of the Soviet Union have helped to make a concerted approach to such threats a practical possibility. Where not long ago the Security Council found itself paralysed in the face of a Soviet veto, there is now a new spirit abroad. In the UN General Assembly, too, countries at one time exercised more by fears of neo-colonialism now look for sanctuary from predators closer at hand. A UN peace-keeping role has become not just more credible, it has actually assumed functions in the field in Cyprus, Lebanon, the Golan Heights, in Central America, with its Angola Verification Mission, and with Good Offices Missions in Afghanistan and Pakistan. The need for their presence is grimly borne out by the statistics: a cost of 761 lives over the years, and 157 of its members arrested and detained last year alone.

East and West therefore have not only a common interest in both a European and a global peace-keeping role; they also seem determined progressively to will the means. Within Europe there is a measure of agreement that the CSCE should become the basis of an effective security framework, involving both the USA and the Soviet Union. In the global context, there is a newly invigorated Security Council able to take decisions more rapidly and compliantly than in the past. Following these paths will also bring more direct means of achieving concertation with the USSR on non-European problems with the minimum delay.

The consequences for defence planning

Defence reviews in all NATO countries have concluded that the new requirement will be for lighter, more mobile forces and equipment. They have anticipated NATO's own review of strategy. Even so, the 1990 NATO summit in London already agreed to field smaller forces, restructured to be highly mobile, and versatile to give maximum flexibility in deciding how to respond to a crisis. Readiness of active units would be scaled back, and there will be greater reliance on the ability to build up rapidly larger forces if and when needed. There are to be multinational corps made up of national units.

Although much of this reduction should in practice be negotiated within the CFE talks, defence budgets have already been trimmed, the debate made public, and the parameters of cuts and restructuring announced. Objectives for reducing US troop levels in Europe, as well as the British Army of the Rhine (BAOR) are fully in the public domain. Even the discussion about nuclear tactical air-to-surface missiles (TASMs) and where to host them is being conducted in the open; what could be more confidence building than that, if the Soviets take it in the right spirit?

What is clear is that even defensive, let alone offensive, systems and force levels will be drastically reduced. In part this will be the dual process of confidence building and mutually negotiated reductions to achieve a stalemate balance at the lowest supportable level; and in part also because NATO members will already have anticipated that process in the knowledge that their electorates want to see the money spent on other things. So the received wisdom is, 'smaller, more flexible, mobile and versatile forces'. In practice, however, caution and the defence establishment have delayed a full revision and, as in most government reviews, cuts are heaviest among those who shout least. In both the UK and the USA, the navy has received little more than an approving glance.

What then are the kind of forces which would best respond to the requirements and challenges discussed above? In fact, they would correspond closely to the description of size, versatility and mobility—not unnaturally, since this is the result of analyses carried out singly and jointly by most countries. It also corresponds with the ultimate force totals as currently predicted. Due to the likelihood that US forces in Europe will eventually be below 50,000, the ceiling of 370,000 for the combined German forces agreed at the Stavropol meeting, and the probability that no foreign troops as such will be stationed in Germany, the size of units maintained by other NATO members is likely to be quite small.

The implications for the organisation of a joint defence force are thereby made more interesting. On the one hand, the concept of multinational corps, composed of separate units from different countries, becomes more attractive (even if some believe that the operational problems are likely to reach levels of celestial comedy; whilst others hold that the more inefficient an army, the less the likelihood of its becoming involved in war). All that is relatively unfamiliar territory which has still to be explored.

At the same time, it brings nearer the concept of role specialisation. Under this, the smaller countries would cease to maintain the full panoply of army, navy and airforce. Those like the UK, invested with an experienced naval force, would compensate for the scrapping of several navies consisting of token ships. The same would apply to other services, which would thus acquire efficiencies not present in largely ceremonial forces.

Both developments will facilitate more effective command structures and integration. This is imperative if units are indeed to be highly mobile, since that requires swift agreement on where and how they are to be moved.

Keeping the peace

As we have seen above, fire-fighting and peace-keeping duties are likely to be the paramount tasks of the restructured forces within the new Europe. To these may be added a number of other emergency or disaster relief operations. One may think of imminent environmental accidents in eastern Europe, of another Chernobyl or Armenian earthquake. All need a combination of highly trained men, of specialised equipment and techniques, of reconnaissance planes, helicopters, recovery vehicles and all the other paraphernalia on which an army moves.

The Belgian Foreign Minister, Mark Eyskens, is father to one of several plans for constituting a pan-European peace-keeping force. His calls for the drawing of troops from both NATO and the Warsaw Pact. This would be a practical as well as a political gesture, though one hopes that the reality of such a force would long outlive the dying Pact. Another such step would be the offer to the Soviet Union and east European countries of joint exercises in crisis management. Few steps could achieve more by way of confidence building than the regular exchanges, contacts, joint objectives and training this implies at a totally constructive and peaceable level.

Rapid deployment, light equipment and multinational compositions are pecisely the qualities required for such peace-keeping and civil defence roles. Although the bulk of the units will initially have no experience of service with the UN peace-keeping forces, attachment to the multinational corps will be a useful preparation for an out-of-area function for which they will need to be equally available.

An essential aspect of peace-keeping must surely be the search for a leak-proof system to control exports and re-exports of arms. Effective force reductions in Europe will in themselves create a spate of surplus weaponry. At the same time the temptation will be great for manufacturers first to seek new outlets and only then to diversify into civilian production.

This is one of a complex of related issues which will require study and concerted action. Stemming the flow of arms to the Third World is one. Another is how peace can be made profitable. What products can replace arms and offer the same profit potential? What new technologies—in consumer goods, in information technology, in genetic and botanical advances—are ready to be phased in? Can the ploughshares so urgently needed to rehabilitate the eastern economies offer enough commercial incentive to redirect the arms industries? Is our free market system capable of adapting to moral choice, as we have lately seen with the introduction of green products?

Equally to be included in such a review, perhaps with the greatest urgency, is the question of nuclear proliferation. Some of the considerations of commercial interest and export safeguards will be the same as for conventional arms. But it will also raise agonising problems for some of the signatories of the one imperfect instrument we have so far, the nuclear non-proliferation treaty. Others are unlikely to be attracted to join unless existing signatories respect their undertakings to reduce their nuclear forces, rather than to increase their destructive power through modernisation.

The transition from confrontation to peace-keeping is a logical process which started with the freeing of eastern Europe, the disintegration of the Warsaw Pact, the receding Soviet threat and the disappearance of the central front. As yet the logic has been only partly absorbed, the consequences far from fully explored. All we know dimly is that the world will never again be quite the same.

We have yet to grasp fully that the problems of peace-keeping—both in and out-of-area—will exert their own compulsion. How to adapt ourselves and our forces is less a matter of choice than of responding to the imperatives of a wholly unfamiliar situation.

5

Helping the Former Enemy

'Mankind today faces unprecedented problems and the future will hang in the balance, if joint solutions are not found.'

MIKHAIL GORBACHEV, *Perestroika*

The German example

Now that the heady events of 1989 are giving way to more sober appraisal, the West finds itself in a dilemma. Just as it had never before had a Cold War, there had never been a 'cold victory'. And whose victory was it anyway? Does it belong to us in the West, who for over forty years made the sacrifices and held the line? Or to the peoples of eastern Europe who for all that time suffered oppression and put up the final struggle? Yet ours undoubtedly is the prize.

Was there ever a time when the vanquished enemy went unpunished? Should we not exact reparations, or put on trial those responsible for countless crimes, as we did in Nuremberg? Will the millions of victims of Stalin, of Honecker and Ceauşescu, not demand to be avenged? Is all the suffering on both sides of the iron curtain to be requited only with belated access to food, capitalism and consumer choice?

What kind of a 'victory' do we in the West have anyway, if we do not at least have the option of marching in there to clean up? After a decent war, you have the chance to put a few things right, man to man, before you go home and get demobbed. Here, the former enemy territory remains out of bounds. And where have all the 'commies' and 'stasis' gone? Have they all suddenly reformed, or have they hidden their leather coats and their torture kits and are just biding their time until the civilians make a hash of it?

And what of the USSR itself? The Communist Party is still there, kept apparently by Mr Gorbachev. The KGB survives and former agents accuse it of conducting its business as usual. We have seen some pictures of prison riots, but who knows how many *gulags* there are still? We estimate how many divisions Gorbachev has, but how many votes would keep him in place if he were to face the ballot box? Ordinary Soviets seem not to care what happens to their patron saint if he fails to put bread and meat in the shops.

All these imponderables offer a rich diet not only to opponents like Boris Yeltsin, but also to our own hawks and doves in the West. It is a strange and unique situation in which we find ourselves, but also an unsettling one. The old certainties of the Cold War have gone, the division of our world into goodies and baddies—with even a few intriguingly ambiguous ones between—is no more. Little wonder that those for whom the excitement has already worn thin feel left rudderless, adrift without a compass on a strong current hurtling us into uncharted seas.

Where then should we be looking for our lodestar? One example which lies to hand is our experience with post-war Germany. It happens to be a convenient one, for there too we felt that peace had to be built on something more positive than revenge. Certainly, the victors cleaned up, and in their various ways—the western allies with judicial process, the Soviets with the same brutality as had been visited upon them—sought to ensure that nothing of the kind should ever happen again.

One great insight, however, was to acknowledge the contribution to the rise of Hitler made by the vengefulness and severity of the victors at Versailles. Though many of the effects were deliberately exaggerated, the demand for wholly unrealistic reparations, the dismantling and shipping abroad of factories and entire industries, had disastrous economic consequences. Unemployment, declining production and spiralling inflation were to provide the fuel for the next global conflagration.

In contrast, the decision to punish the criminals, but not a whole people, has proved itself both just and effective. The wisdom of Solomon displayed by the allies was perfected with the concept of the Marshall Plan, the utterly enlightened US initiative to lend Europe— including the defeated Germany—the money with which to rebuild its ruined economies. True that shortly thereafter the Cold War provided an additional compulsion to put Germany back on her feet, and even to rearm her. Yet the vision of the western allies—at Potsdam, if not at

Yalta—at length resulted not only in peace in the West, but also in its mounting prosperity.

Politically, too, the dividends have been handsome. Acceptance of the West German people and their new and vigorous democracy into the comity of nations made it possible together to build the European Community. Then as now, the only solution to the 'German question' was to seek its integration into a larger common entity, and one in which the loss of West Germany's ability to act independently would result in a positive pooling—rather than loss—of sovereignty by the others. The development of the EC since then, its progress from trade and agriculture into virtually all areas of public activity, has been a gradual adjustment of that pooling to what its members collectively regarded as an acceptable level.

Interesting to note that, throughout more than thirty years of the EC's existence, West Germany has invariably been on the side of progressive integration. Even today, when many are afraid of a united Germany striking out alone, its government is insisting on a rapid deepening and consolidation of the EC in its newly determined directions of economic and monetary as well as political union.

Significantly, the main impulse for European integration came from France, which had suffered most from German aggression and had most to lose from any repetition. If Jean Monnet was the architect of the Community, Robert Schuman was the builder who laid the foundation. His concept of the European Coal and Steel Community, precursor of the EC, was designed very simply to integrate Germany's reviving heavy industry with that of the rest of western Europe, to make an omelette which no one could unscramble. Units in one country became dependent on supplies from another, production targets became jointly fixed and controlled, and overnight the ability of any one country to build up an independent war capacity had vanished.

How to treat with the Soviet Union

The lessons of history are many, but they are not always shown to us with great clarity. Only rarely is one able to see some incontrovertible truth, some shining example, stand out from its pages. The case of Germany surely is one; the EC may well prove to be another.

What consequences would flow if we were to adopt the German model in our present stance towards the Soviet Union? All of us seem agreed that our first priority is to demonstrate to the Soviets that the

West has no aggressive intent. Much has already been done to achieve this: treaties for nuclear and conventional force reductions, the two-plus-four framework which settled the future of Germany, continuation of the Helsinki process and institutionalising the CSCE into a co-operative instrument to sustain democracy and keep the peace, even invitations to Mr Gorbachev to attend NATO and Group of Seven summits. But, in addition, there is still the most significant, if least defined: a Conference on Security Building Measures (CSBM).

All these are intended to be meeting points which will remain in continuous session until their work is done. It follows that the West is looking for a continual reduction in the threat which one side presents to the other; for the development of trust and confidence; and for a sustained movement towards common institutions within which the maintenance of peace and the building of prosperity will become a co-operative enterprise.

The Soviet leaders appear to have grasped that the West has no immediate hostile intent, even though they have seen the global power balance tilt inexorably to their disadvantage. That implies that a good measure of confidence already exists; but confidence is a volatile commodity which needs constantly to be nurtured. In addition to doing that, are there ways in which we can build on their present mood for more positive ends? Is it possible that, rather than just pursuing our own agenda, we can offer to help them with theirs?

Glasnost has ensured that we can read their problems, as well as those of Mr Gorbachev personally. It is plain to see that, in whatever manner they choose to approach the problem of building a more efficient economy, their immediate need is for a number of highly specific commodities: they need food; they need advice on how to grow it, harvest it, store it, transport it and market it; they need the technical and physical inputs to do all these things. Europe and the USA, the most successful agricultural producers in the world, possess all the knowledge that is needed, and an abundance of the materials to go with it. They also have the surpluses to ship some temporary food supplies to set the whole chain in motion.

We have for so long regarded the USSR as the most powerful adversary on earth, that we are now surprised to find it at one and the same time a superpower and a developing country. It is precisely that paradox which has made its breath falter in the race to maintain superpower status. It now needs time and peace to achieve its economic development.

The hallmark of a developing country is stagnation. Invariably there is a vicious circle of low productivity: nothing in the shops to provide a work incentive; minimal purchasing power; no market for either farmer or manufacturer. Government policies do their bit to distort and aggravate the picture further, but generally at a more advanced level. What we have seen in the Revolution of 1989—and are now witnessing as a consequence in many parts of Africa—is in part the revolt of a populace too long denied the human right to be decently fed and housed. All of them had been promised that Marxism offered the one true road by which they would be. All except their opulent leaders have been disappointed.

Now it is up to the West to see that capitalism does not disillusion them just as much—either because it proves too hard to generate it by themselves; or, more gravely, because it lacks the human quality to respond to their needs. As one western diplomat remarked after a crucial NATO meeting, 'We stretched out our hand, but the hand was empty; we have got to put something into this hand.'

The UK and the US were originally opposed to economic aid to the USSR, the one because it believed that the free-market systems are not yet there to ensure its effectiveness, the other because it claimed that to take the pressure off the economy would be to subsidise the military. Both arguments depend upon one's point of view, and both can be successfully challenged, as US food credits have since demonstrated. As with Third World problems, economists can argue their corner long and convincingly, yet none of them has ever been able to avoid the next famine. In the last analysis, should not our starting point be the consistency of western policy?

If that were so, confidence building would take the same paramount position in economic matters that it has been given in the security field. Inconsistency and conflicting signals are surely a way of undermining rather than enhancing confidence. And how is confidence served by a public debate on the best way to keep up the economic pressure which brought the USSR to its knees?

The Soviet economy

The inefficiencies in the Soviet system are plain to see. In his highly critical appraisal of the ills of the Soviet economy, Mr Gorbachev himself has said that the USSR is consuming far more by way of raw materials, energy and other resources per unit of output than any other industrial country.

If food is the key, the problem begins with the inability of the transport and distribution systems to ensure that what is produced reaches the shops. Some 30–40 per cent of food is lost in this way, compounding the inefficiencies of production and black marketeering. Other bottlenecks are capital and technology, urgent in themselves to replace antiquated and pollutant industries, vital for the process of turning the war machine to peaceful and productive uses.

Consumption levels in the USSR are variously estimated; the most optimistic source places them close to those in Mexico and Portugal. But it is clear that defence retrenchment and dislocations are leading to a decline in industrial output. In 1990 it fell by over 1 per cent, GNP by 3 per cent and exports by 12 per cent. In 1991 production is expected to have fallen a further 1.5 per cent. There is hard evidence of troop withdrawals and demobilisation, of weapons being scrapped, and of plants being converted to civilian uses. There is even a decision to match the reduction of generals in the Pentagon by giving one-third of Soviet generals in the armed forces and the Defence Ministry their marching orders over the coming months.

Too little is known conclusively about the Soviet economy. The only data available had up to now been pieced together by the intelligence community, despite concealment and disinformation. That is about to change. In an unprecedented move following the Houston economic summit, the government opened its books for an audit conducted by the International Monetary Fund (IMF) and the World Bank. As a first step, this has provided basic data on the state of the economy and allowed a judgement on where the change and first aid need to be applied.

Much more importantly, the audit should provide an overview of how resources move through the system into various sectors, and hence the extent to which they are fungible as between civilian and military uses. Once that arterial system is charted, it should be a short step to a mechanism for control and verification of any externally injected funds. Access by the USSR to membership of both multilateral institutions, as well as of the European Bank for Reconstruction and Development, will in any event entail keeping the books open and accepting a degree of advice and supervision.

Anticipating this, some reforms are already being implemented. Jointly and individually, the West has pointed out that no freeing of trade or investment is possible unless the rouble is made fully convertible. Limited steps to give Soviet enterprises access to foreign exchange have now been taken. Similarly—although there is as yet no provision for privatising any significant public undertakings—small businesses can now be owned individually. Capitalism has been established at the grass roots—a move of potentially more far-reaching significance than the selling off of state monopolies which no one is yet in a position to buy, let alone to operate. But the way has also been cleared for foreign companies, in joint ventures as well as wholly-owned enterprises.

It may well be that indecisiveness over reform has thrown the economy into chaos. Yet, thanks to invigilation by the IMF and World Bank, it may also become more transparent. Although there is evidence that substantial military equipment is still being produced—it would be surprising if it were not—the scale and extent should in future be capable of being directly monitored.

If self-analysis is any guide, Mr Gorbachev has already provided the answer. In his book *Perestroika*[3] he writes, 'The principal priorities are known to lie in a profound structural reorganisation of the economy, in reconstruction of its material base, in new technologies, in investment policy changes, and in high standards of management. All that adds up to one thing—acceleration of scientific and technological progress.'

Why should we help?

There are as many answers to that question as the people one asks. Reconciliation, humanitarian grounds, emergency aid, solidarity, political favours, support for democratic movements, economic reform, supporting Mikhail Gorbachev, even helping Boris Yeltsin. All of these are valid, and some will already have been proved effective. The bill for German unification and membership of NATO, for instance, is certainly not limited to a ceiling on its combined forces. Much aid will flow, even if Mr Gorbachev's rejection of political strings is prudently respected.

Yet all these answers ignore one important beneficiary—ourselves.

It is a feature of such debates to strike righteous attitudes and lose sight of the main chance. Surely it cannot be our objective to see the Soviet Union develop a market economy for no better reason than to allow us to justify pumping in money. Nor can it be our purpose to keep them teetering on the poverty line so as to throttle their military expenditures (do we not also have a vested interest in a strong Soviet Union, rather than one on the edge of bankruptcy?). Still less do we want them to continue to eye longingly our prosperity, with the nannyish admonition that, if they behave themselves, they may one day be allowed to share in it.

Would not our interest be better served by showing them that—despite the Marxist nostrums—capitalism can work for them too? And could that not mean that we have a duty to ourselves to go in there and make it happen? What with the US budget deficit, with the depletions of overseas debt and internal banking crises brought on our own heads by deregulation, and with our perennial obligations to the developing world, we may well feel that we do not have much money to take care of the USSR as well. But that would mean being hoist by our own arguments. If the systems in the Soviet Union are restricting its reconstruction, it is not principally money that is needed but know-how. And that could lever significant mutual advantages at minimum cost.

Some options for the West

There is more than one shopping list of what the West might do to provide timely help to the Soviet government—be it Gorbachev, Yeltsin or a person or persons as yet unknown. A number of plans have been devised and advertised. Some are ambitious, others perhaps too modest in scale. Taken together, they offer the advantage to those willing to help that everyone can choose according to his capacity, so long as there is some co-ordination among them.

The chief need is clearly to tender advice on making existing economic structures work more efficiently. In the macro-economic sense this will be done by the IMF and World Bank. At operational levels there is scope for everything from agricultural economists to plant and process engineers. It will always remain for the Soviet government to decide on the pace and extent of economic reform; what the West can do is to offer practical advice, backed up with the people who can help to implement it.

If we believe what we say about liberating the energies of the private sector, a progressive improvement in the operation of the economy, and concurrently in the policy environment, should encourage western firms to take an interest in co-operative arrangements with Soviet enterprises. High on the list would be candidates for early privatisation, which is unlikely to be long delayed. We have witnessed the long road to re-establishing private property rights in other east European countries, and no one will be surprised if the flow of investment is slow when it eventually comes. Yet there are already signs of active Japanese interest in the Russian Federation, whilst German industry is gaining footholds in banking and service industries which will be strategically placed for participations when the time arrives.

It would be idle to pretend that the Soviet Union is likely to become a flourishing capitalist economy in a short time. Putting significant resources into a foetal private sector hemmed in by 70 million bureaucrats has already disillusioned a number of western companies. But there are very substantial opportunities just in making major state concerns work more efficiently—in the oil industry, in transport and telecommunications, and above all in nuclear safety.

There are other fields which deserve attention, both by the Soviets and the West. The whole area of labour relations, of social policy, of ineffectual trade unions, of wage-bargaining—in short, of post-Communist Party diktat—will need examination and reform.

There too are specialised western organisations qualified to help with the design of new structures. There can be hardly an area of economic or social activity which is not in need at the very least of an overhaul, if not of complete modernisation and restructuring.

More ambitiously, there is the development of the Soviet Union's rich energy resources. The Dutch Prime Minister, Ruud Lubbers, has called for the creation of a European Energy Community embracing Soviet and east European oil, coal and natural gas resources. For the producer countries, such a community would ensure the transfer of vitally needed capital and technology to improve production and marketing. For western Europe it would mean avoiding an energy dependence on other more volatile supplier countries. For both combined, it would offer the beginning of the benefits of coupling their economies. Above all, in security terms it would have some of the same effect as the one-time European Coal and Steel Community.

It should be in our immediate interest to seek more such couplings, to integrate the economies of East and West within a new Europe. The joint venture between Aeroflot and British Airways is pointing the way. But they need not be confined to the economic sphere. There are equally good and urgent opportunities in education, in training, in law and the judiciary, in parliamentary affairs, in cultural co-operation and exchanges. Each one of these can become a vehicle for nurturing the habit of co-operation and the development of trust.

In an age where the Soviet President is taking lessons from White House staff on how to run the Kremlin, and his foreign minister takes part in the deliberations of the NATO Council, the possibilities are manifest.

Opportunities in the security field

The opening of military installations on both sides, reciprocal visits of senior staff officers, exchanges of information on manoeuvres and the presence of observers have already demonstrated how far it is possible to go in a short time in lowering the barriers. Successive CFE negotiations will undoubtedly confirm an agreed open skies and open door policy to facilitate verification to the maximum. The CSCE arrangements, too, will be developing their own control and verification procedures. Undoubtedly, there will be an interim period during which full verification is not physically possible. There is already agreement that where this is inescapable, matters will have to be taken on trust. Perhaps that is the best indication yet of how far the process of confidence building has advanced.

In the politico-military field, too, the events in the Persian Gulf will have served to give both sides useful insights into the preparedness and dispositions of naval and mobile units. Unprecedentedly, the Soviet Union has handed over information on the arming and guidance mechanisms of the missiles it sold to Iraq. Whilst the time may not be ripe for sending joint task forces to such areas, it cannot be far off. In any event, there has been considerable co-ordination of a joint approach within the Security Council, as well as the fullest information on allied moves and contingency plans.

These developments have plainly exhibited a number of new characteristics on the part of the Soviet leadership. First, an abandonment of the policy of mischief, which dictated automatic support for whoever was embarrassing the West, and the return to a normal reaction to aggression. If it was Khrushchev who claimed that peace was indivisible, Gorbachev at long last acknowledged it. Secondly, the possibility of aligning Soviet and western objectives and developing agreed responses in an emergency. Thirdly, the subordination of military reflexes to political imperatives. Fourthly, a rejection of new imbroglios in Third World affairs. Fifthly, and most importantly, the display of a pattern of responsible behaviour and the foreswearing of all former aggressiveness and polemics.

From these characteristics one may deduce that there is now an underlying identity of overall objectives between the USSR and the West. Both wish to be left in peace, from each other as well as the outside world. Both are anxious to reduce the defence burden on their economies. Both are willing to demonstrate that they have no designs upon the other and are prepared to open some of their arsenals and installations to inspection.

In these circumstances it is almost as if the Soviets were inviting their former adversaries to go still further in probing their good intentions. So long as fairness and parity are maintained, there seems currently no end to what might not be proposed and accepted to confirm that goodwill. The sooner that trust is complete, it seems, the quicker the Soviets can get on with their internal business and restructuring.

It would therefore be prudent for the West to consider other proposals which would satisfy the common objectives of developing trust and avoiding a future return to international delinquency. Nations, like individuals, respond to the responsibilities placed upon them; ostracise them, or leave them to their own devices, and they can all too easily develop behavioural problems. For all we know, there may not be much time before internal preoccupations once more force the USSR onto a less friendly course.

The most crucial part of the peace process is to reduce tension. Hence the nuclear accords, the CFE treaty, the Helsinki process and the development of the CSCE. All these processes are basically agreed and are taking their course. Now may therefore be the time for an even more imaginative leap.

The needs of the Soviet economy have been argued above. They could easily lead to a deal with the West for making Soviet industry more efficient—a kind of managerial Marshall Plan. At first this would involve primarily technical assistance and very little capital. Its main direction would be to help what there is to function, and thus to give an immediate stimulus to production at the same time as organising proper channels of distribution.

The second priority would be to achieve technological improvements. This will require investment in new plant and processes, but time, trust and reforms will by then have moved on to make possible a more informed judgement on where the capital should come from. It seems fairly predictable that the supplier countries would, as always, be ready to provide the necessary credits—so long as the economy was sufficiently in gear to make repayment credible.

In any event, the object of introducing new technology will be to achieve more with less. This is the hallmark of western industry and perhaps the main argument why a depressed economy should seek foreign assistance with its rehabilitation. The USSR has indisputable areas of excellence—witness only its space programme—but the great

bulk of industrial infrastructure is archaic as well as under-utilised.
'Our rockets can find Halley's comet and fly to Venus with amazing
accuracy,' says Mr Gorbachev disarmingly, 'but . . . there are difficulties in the supply of foodstuffs, housing, consumer goods and
services.'[4]

The 'more-with-less' principle has particular applications in the
defence industry. In common with other industries, it greatly
improves the economics of production, thus reducing the need for
swollen defence expenditures. Beyond that, it provides greater efficiency to what is produced. Breakdowns are reduced with quality
production; but improved maintenance technology can dramatically
cut down-times, thus achieving the same operational efficiency with a
smaller inventory.

Other defence-related benefits can be introduced in addition to
production and maintenance teams. In the circumstances envisaged,
it is perhaps not too far-fetched to think of a measure of standardisation between Soviet and western equipment. This could be entirely
feasible on peripherals. A degree of common procurement of non-
sensitive items would become a logical step, bringing additional
economies of scale. Above all, the management of the whole of the
engineering branches, from transport systems to workshops, could
benefit from such a transfer of skills.

Futuristic as this sounds, there are several highly practical reasons
why such co-operation could be feasible. The first is economic necessity. Secondly, it is a natural extension of assistance with civilian fields
of production. If intentions were to turn bellicose once more, agriculture and other industries would at once become strategic too.
However, if the future is to be the pursuit of common objectives, and
within a common security system, there would be sound arguments
for a measure of standardisation in design, production and main-
tenace of equipment, particularly if used in future only for common
purposes. Direct involvement in these areas can also be seen as a
natural progression of the process begun with inspection and verification of arms accords.

Most Soviets understand that their security problems are not
caused by Polish cavalry or German panzers, but by the inefficiencies
of their own industrial system. The next step would be to encourage
them to diagnose their problems in terms of where the West can help.

A final but conclusive argument is that, so long as the nuclear
deterrent exists, shared confidences are an insurance policy for both
sides. That, after all, was the point which made all current military

understandings possible. There seems no reason why it should not continue to provide a useful base for further improvements and accommodations.

What we can achieve

All this may seem utopian; and yet it is a step certainly no farther than that which we have already taken from the depths of the Cold War to where we are today. Audacious, yes. Difficult to negotiate, maybe. Ambiguous and open to misinterpretation, only if our diplomacy is more feeble than it has any right to be.

The case for technical and managerial assistance in industry and agriculture is compelling, especially as an invaluable part of the confidence building process. Why then should we not take a hand in the military machine as well? It would represent a further step in the agreed direction of reducing tension. Make it reciprocal, by all means. There will be dozens of ways in which we can give the Soviets equal access to our own establishments, from in-plant training to stationed observers.

One of the most effective means of avoiding war-like blunders is to have defence systems and structures which both sides are able to understand. That must include the objectives for which it is built and the commands by which it is activated. If we can help our old adversary to build such a system, and make all the wrinkles in ours plain for him to see, we shall be increasing his security as well as our own.

The principal gains will be mutual trust and common security. Some food aid, a deal of technical assistance, a little capital and some sharing of yesterday's secrets seems a fairly modest price to pay. It is a package well within our means. For us to wait until big money is required would risk impoverishing ourselves. We would then also be giving further forfeits to Japan as the financier of the western deficit.

In Moscow the class struggle has been declared dead. Marxism has been reinterpreted to mean 'All humanity working together to solve common problems.' Let us see if, at long last, there is some truth in that. The formula has been tried and tested with Germany. The Soviet Union was never so bitter an enemy.

6

The Illusion of Frontiers

'Space is the most constant stake of human conflicts.'

RAYMOND ARON, *Peace and War*

Of frontiers and security zones

War, by definition, is the violation of frontiers. Since time immemorial warring tribes, then nations, have sought sweeter grass beyond their confines, or greatness in dominion over their neighbours. All wars have had the acquisition of territory as their principal motivation. From Cain to Korea, from poisoned arrows to the atomic age, the ambition of man and his armouries has been to expand his possessions.

Not unnaturally, a host of other motives have been invoked. The righting of injustices, the liberation of minorities, the reclaiming of lost provinces, the need for security, the uprooting of heresies and the restoration of religious or ideological orthodoxy, the right of a master or more enlightened race to rule. Essentially, however, there was but one objective—aggrandisement of the aggressor's status or resources.

The colonial age brought the benign intents of civilising the savage, conversion to Christian principles, peaceable trading unhindered by local irruptions, and establishing protectorates over tribes warring among themselves. It proved a golden era where all the spoils of war could often be had without conquest or passage of arms. Indeed, the bitterest rivals in Europe were able to divide such freely available territory and strike gentlemanly deals for its disposition. For well over a century, the tools of Lycées and the London Missionary Society proved as effective at pacification as gunboats and grenadiers.

In vain has history tried to teach that greatness brings only insecurity, for it invariably excites envy, the desire for revenge and recovery of the alienated spoils. Sometimes the harvest is swift, as with the recapturing of German-occupied territories; sometimes long-drawn out, with losses and regains, as in the Hundred Years War; and on occasion history can hold its breath for centuries, as with colonial independence.

Yet over time there have been changes. The warring of Greek city-states, according to David Hume, 'had more in view the honour of leading the rest, than any well-grounded hopes of authority and dominion'.[5] Roman campaigns, whilst equally gentlemanly in comparison with medieval pillages, were for the pure glory of conquest, and the joy of expanding the limits of the civilised globe. By the early 19th century, Clausewitz was able to liken war instead of 'to any Art, to business competition, which is also a conflict of human interests and activities; and it is still more like State policy, which again may be looked upon as a kind of business competition on a great scale'.[6]

With that analogy, he was able to forecast the transition from classic engagements to modern warfare. Preparation for a single engagement that would decide everything, he prognosticated, will lead to absolute war. How right he was proved, and how accurate is his prediction of today's situation in which overkill arsenals are ranged against each other.

There have, in consequence, been other changes. Particularly within Europe, the absolute interdiction of the desire to own space has given way to the need to control it. Buffer zones, border strips, no-man's land, occupied forward areas, whole vassal states such as the non-Soviet Warsaw Pact countries, much of the Soviet empire ranged around its central borders, all have become the order of the day. But so have Monroe Doctrines and spheres of influence, tacit or formally recognised, which are deemed to give legitimate assurance of a major country's security.

True that the raw conquests of Genghis Khan still have their contemporary parallels in Korea, Vietnam, Cambodia and Iraq. From that we may infer that war is in some way linked with the state of development of a society and the symbols by which it recognises its own values. Yet one may also conclude that, in the absence of any law between states where tensions exist, the former have at least come to a recognition of mutual security needs, whilst the latter hope still to be able to profit from that very state of lawlessness. Whilst Third World countries are still at the stage of St Augustine, of 'Yes, Lord, but not yet', those in Europe—which have so notably bloodied themselves—

have come to acknowledge that peace is a greater virtue than war.

The ambiguity of frontiers is both cause and effect of the security zone concept. Causal is the fact that, three times in recent history German generals have proved that frontiers have no validity. Moreover, on the two most recent occasions, they have shown that the frontier between them and their adversary is not necessarily the chosen route. Neutral or non-belligerent neighbours have become the passage to circumvent heavily fortified borders. Their frontiers were violated in order to achieve incursions into France from undefended directions.

Non-aggression pacts have had an equally equivocal history. More often than not they have proved the prelude to plunder of the very object they solemnly undertook to protect. The Munich agreement meant the abandonment of Czechoslovakia, 'like a sausage to be sliced up by all who cared to help themselves', in Mussolini's famous phrase. The 1934 Polish-German Treaty was to be the next casualty, the dismembering of Poland by Germany and the USSR made feasible by the famous non-aggression pact between them, itself to be broken only months later by Hitler's invasion of the Soviet Union.

A further rationale for security zones is the ubiquity and mobility of modern forces. Air transport, of men and even their heaviest equipment, has meant that troops can arrive rapidly at any forward base or bridgehead. Carrier-borne aircraft can extend the capacity of aerial penetration, its depth increased by flight refuelling. If fifty years ago blitzkrieg meant the rapid advance of motorised columns with forward air support, today we have the ability to make instant war—even without the launching of all-out nuclear attack.

The consequences of security zones are equally novel. A real border may be meticulously defined, yet the crossing of a far more nebulous line, deliberately unrecognised in any formal way, will already be considered aggression. Until the Berlin Wall came down, and East German border guards disappeared along the 900 km frontier, the Iron Curtain marked that absolute touch-me-not line. For the USA, as the Soviet Union discovered in 1962 and on subsequent occasions, it lies in Cuba and Nicaragua—as well as considerably farther off its eastern shore. For, with whatever buffers nations may aim to surround themselves, the existence of the outer perimeter must eventually become equivalent to the inner.

Forward strategy in essence is nothing but the recognition that frontiers cannot be defended. It deals with what lies beyond them, what can be expected to be thrown at them, and how to go about preempting that. Only in the 19th century thinking of the architects of the Maginot and Siegfried Lines is there the concept of a fixed line of first defence. Modern warfare—God forbid—demands that the front begins as deep inside enemy territory as possible.

The political significance

The implications of this evolution are that the real front line today lies not along frontiers but in capitals. The *cordon sanitaire*, the line of first defence, does not follow the Oder-Neisse or the Mekong, the Sakhalins or the Mediterranean—it lies in Moscow and Hanoi and Tripoli. It is there that the political battles must be fought which, with the exception of brush-fire wars, are the only ones still open to a modern state. For the truth is that war as a means of gaining territory, or of protecting one's business in the Clausewitz sense, is no longer an option for certain states.

The reasons for nuclear powers not to resort to war with each other are clear and have been examined elsewhere. They rule out the entire European theatre, the United States and all of its closest allies, including Japan. However, the prohibition derives not from geography or alliances but from strength and political status. Thus for the NATO powers, as ultimately for the USSR, it extends worldwide. Conventional wars can no longer be launched on their own initiative in Africa or the western hemisphere, in Asia or the Pacific.

Perhaps the earliest triumph of western social and political thought was its avid adoption by those it was developed to protect. The curbing of child labour resulted in trade unions. Championing of racial equality led both to emancipation and to black power. Protection of minorities has brought claims for separate development. Liberal-socialist thought resulted in colonial independence and rejection of those who gave life to its principles. Even the abolition of caning in schools brought child action. Thus it seems that the struggle for equality can coalesce only once the guiding ideas have been formed by those responsible for the original inequality. The protection of the weaker is an interaction between their endurance and its recognition by more advanced groups among the stronger.

But the trigger for action lies within the awakening conscience of the strong. It follows that western thought generates a succession of inhibitors restricting its actions. There is an interim period during which they may still be transgressed, incurring only domestic opprobrium. But once they are adopted by those whom they concern, they rapidly pass into the domain of international standards. Then we can witness the strange spectacle of nations which have recognised the error of past ways being pilloried for what they have out of their own conscience abjured. They become arraigned ex-post facto under new standards which they have themselves donated to the world.

The import for military actions is that policing remains permissible, punitive action not. Time and again we have been faced with the searing choice of how to deal with an overseas aggressor. The options become doubly painful where some western strategic or economic interest is involved, such as Kuwait or the Falklands, and policing is not solely for the protection of the far-off aggrieved. In Korea and Vietnam we were still concerned with the protection of the free world, and allowed ourselves to get bogged down excruciatingly in the search for the kind of decisive engagement which had passed into history with the Second World War. We now know that the frontiers of the free world lie elsewhere.

The front line, indeed, passes not only through the capitals of potential adversaries. It makes several turns also around the United Nations and other fora involving friend and foe. Where once one would have marshalled confederates and invoked alliances, today the first step is to mobilise world opinion and to neutralise potential dissent. That is a task of diplomacy, and Clausewitz may still be right where its final purpose is approbation for launching a multinational force against an aggression already committed. But most of the time a resolution of condemnation will prove sufficient for both sides.

The pace and pattern of diplomacy have also been radically altered. Today we are familiar with the spectacle of heads of government consulting and briefing each other over their hotlines, then despatching their foreign ministers to concert and negotiate. Diplomacy and negotiation have become one, and ambassadors serve mostly to create the climate propitious to rapid understanding between both countries when the need arises.

A potent agent in bringing about the interdiction of force is the advance of information technology. In olden times the delays in transmitting information provided convenient cover for campaigns to be launched before the world became aware of them and could muster counter-measures and opinion pressures. Today the knowledge is immediate, both of action and reaction. Information, too, fails to recognise frontiers.

The same is true of technology generally. The scientific and technology community is linked worldwide. Common research projects, publication of results, academic exchanges, access to international data bases all ensure that the frontiers of knowledge remain only those yet to be conquered. Once translated into hardware, governments or communities may still aim to preserve their own security by restricting their use and export. But availability of the basic knowledge, and the multiplicity of sources originating it, will quickly lead to similar technology being developed elsewhere. The Greek axiom that a thought once formulated cannot be recalled, has been abundantly proved true.

Minorities—nations without frontiers

If war for the conquest of space in Europe is no more, its legacies still survive. Populations living in the desired space were generally of no consequence. They could mostly be subdued with a handful of warriors and eventually become a useful source of vassals and mercenaries. Before the great patriotic wars, fighting was a business for professionals. Populations had to endure their battles and pillages, but were often not emotionally engaged in either the campaign or its outcome.

In modern times this radically changed. The nation state excited loyalties and called upon patriotic support. It raised levies and exacted contributions for its wars and its defence. It staked out borders, no longer just for commerce but for protection, and made claims on neighbouring territory where the lines were inconvenient. In times of crisis, whoever was not for it was held to be against it.

Occupied territories were thus suddenly found to be full of recalcitrant populations, treacherous in the ardour of their patriotism, unwilling to concede defeat even when their former government did. As time wore on, they became more politicised and, motivated by their retained identity, ready to demonstrate for their community rights. Long after the annexation, all at once there was a minority problem.

War thus had the effect of creating minorities unable to live in the same space with immigrants and colonisers. Ironically, those who fled and rejoined their former mother country sometimes suffered the same rejection. Yet on both sides they clung even more tenaciously to their old identities, insisting on the exercise of their own rites and customs even in the face of persecution.

Emigrés like the Huguenots and those fortunate enough to escape Hitler or the advancing Soviets, have found it relatively simple to blend into their country of adoption. It is where whole populations are transferred from one jurisdiction to another that minority problems become acute. The dissolution of the Habsburg Empire and the redistribution of its territory after the First World War gave rise to one such wave in modern times. The aftermath of the Second World War was the cause of further traumas, though many of them were rapidly subdued under the successor communist regimes.

Today, as the Soviet Union's security zone dissolves and the oppressive regimes have departed, the map is once more laid bare. What we see is the surviving patchwork of minorities incarcerated within countries which have either remained hostile to them or developed new animosities in line with their agitation for special treatment, consideration or even territorial rights.

We suddenly find before us a map of Europe on which frontiers delineate states but not nations. We can clearly see the tensions developing, almost predict mathematically where fevers will rise as ethnic attractions, for long subdued, spring to new life. We are witnessing a Europe of nations artificially divided, nations which have no frontiers of their own and which increasingly reject those which have been drawn through them. That too is a reality of the new Europe, and a challenge to the wisdom of its new leaders.

Perceptions of sovereignty

Limitations on the ability to use war as an extension of policy, the ambiguity of frontiers, the refusal of knowledge and technology to remain within our grasp, all raise questions about our sovereignty and autonomy. Perceptions of their essential quality already vary widely. So does a valuation of what remains to us.

In essence, sovereignty is equated with the defence of the 'national interest'. However, that at once raises a contradiction, for the national interest is rarely definable in terms of private or corporate interest. Often the two are in conflict, since to invoke it is usually a prelude to sacrifices and restrictions. On the other hand, it has proved a useful device for rallying loyalties despite such discomforts by demonstrating the existence of a higher call upon our allegiance. This is aroused with concepts such as security and national honour. Since these are considered absolutes, it follows that they are not necessarily identified with a ruling party but with a government that becomes, in moments of crisis, the spokesman for all the people.

Sovereignty, for the generation which still remembers the cost of defending it, is a precious commodity central to their own view of the civilised world. It embraces values and ideals still owing much to the Victorians and the role which Britain was able to play in bringing them to other populations. No doubt the same is true of the USA who inherited that role. And therein already lies an irony, for defence of freedom, and the involvement of the USA in it, certainly cost us as much sovereignty as it preserved. The realisation that no one today is able to defend his values unaided, and the complexities and uncertainties of the processes involved, tend towards disillusionment, disengagement and, collectively, to isolationism.

Not so their sons and grandsons. Their perceptions are of open frontiers, of movement without hindrance, of minimum restrictions, of a world without barriers from Berlin to Bangkok. Sovereignty and patriotism are equated with history books, records of mankind's failures to seize the opportunities for personal freedom on offer within its universe. They are held as concepts to legitimise restrictions and regulations, to keep people in and others out, to protect illusory advantages.

Such views are not necessarily those of hippies and loafers, of those seduced by the poppies of Chieng Mai or the mores of California. They require a deal of courage, for the opportunities sought have no value unless they are reciprocal, unless others can settle as easily in my home town and compete for my job. They also mean that, exactly like the old freedoms, they need to be protected with vigilance and expanded with ardour. They have turned out to be as indivisible as freedom ever was. And, as throughout history, they are themselves only steps along a road that has to be travelled with hope and resolve, for it leads into the unknown.

In essence, sovereignty is a concept used to legitimise the actions of governments. The first duty of government is to defend the realm. The second is to guarantee the liberty of its subjects. Paradoxically the evidence is that, in practice, the first has consistently militated against the second. A call to arms has automatically meant the suspension of large areas of civil liberties. Conscription and the war machine of necessity took over for the duration of the emergency. The defence of freedom invariably called for its temporary suppression.

It is debatable whether it did not also lead to fundamental longer term modifications. A belief in the efficacy of command structures tends to be carried over into peace time, leading to dirigiste policies and great absurdities in administration, such as the attempt to tackle food production like a large-scale military exercise as was the case in

East Africa with the Tanganyika groundnuts scheme. In the East, fifty years of paramilitarism has only now collapsed under its own weight. In the West, the need to maintain a credible bulwark to resist the Cold War, and a deterrent against a 'hot' one, created a paradox: the NATO treaty—guarantor of the integrity of the western alliance and its member states—also deprived them of a large measure of individual sovereignty: if any one of them is attacked, the others no longer have a choice but to act in the common interest.

The treaty was the first formal recognition of two facts which had become starkly clear during the Second World War: no single country was any longer able to provide for its own defence; and the countries under threat were not like small principalities huddling under the wings of a protective superpower, but formed an economic system whose prosperity was vital to its political survival. Hence the effort to rebuild western Europe, to reintegrate West Germany and to consolidate the European Community.

The driving force of western economic integration, and the need for managing the world economy became widely accepted. Institutions began to grow apace. With the post-war recovery process completed, the institution responsible widened its horizons, became the Organisation for Economic Co-operation and Development (OECD) and henceforth the forum of the leading economies, with full US and Canadian—and eventually Japanese—membership. The European Coal and Steel Community and Euratom, and finally the European Economic Community itself, gave permanent status to their members acting in partnership and equality, set on the road to 'ever closer union'.

The dim recognition that, whilst the industrial countries sought mutual support, the poorer countries were propelled into independence led to a parallel concern with overseas development. As new countries sought membership, the United Nations became their spokesman and its offshoots, the World Bank and International Monetary Fund as well as its specialised agencies, increasingly focused on their problems. So did the General Agreement on Tariffs and Trade, in addition to its function of arbiter of fair trade between those who still accounted for the great bulk of it. Development aid became a recognised part of the OECD's monitoring of the economies of what were by now the donor countries.

Membership of most, but by no means all, these bodies rests upon treaty obligations which, in practice, can be overridden by force majeure. However, there is a body of international law, enshrined in

Conventions duly ratified by national parliaments, which has entered into domestic law. And in some cases there is enabling legislation which gives laws made elsewhere the force and effect of national legislation. Where then do we stand with our sovereignty?

The bulk of our defence policy and capability is subordinated to NATO. Within the areas covered by NATO, its use is no longer the subject of a sovereign decision: we are required to take up arms on behalf of any one of our 15 allies, whilst submitting our own responses to a consensus reached with them.

Our trade policy has for long been ceded to the EC, first in the field of common tariffs, progressively in agriculture and competition, from 1993 onwards all matters affecting the movement of goods, capital, persons and employment throughout the Community.

The great debate about retaining an independent monetary policy continues. In the meantime the chief instruments—interest rates, exchange rates—are effectively subordinated to the financial markets and the behaviour of the deutschmark and the dollar. What happens in Frankfurt is immediately reflected in London through the integration already achieved by money markets.

In the European Single Act, EC members are already pledged to strive for common foreign policies and to seek to speak with a single voice in international bodies. A separate secretariat already exists for the purpose.

Further steps to harmonise foreign, economic and social policies are already in train. The attempt to make them lead to full economic and political union over a measurable time is being charted.

Central to all this is the field of law. The majority of western countries regard themselves bound by the UN's Universal Declaration of Human Rights; but European governments have acceded to the much more far-reaching European Convention, backed up by the European Court of Human Rights. EC members are also subject to the rulings of the European Court. Both the European agencies offer the right of appeal against abuses of human rights and contraventions of Community laws, especially in the social field. Thus UK nationals are able to seek protection outside of—and indeed in defiance of—British courts.

But the treaty of accession to the EC also gave priority to Community law over national law in the areas of competence of the Rome Treaty. This means that all laws and regulations emanating from Brussels, in myriad fields, pass more or less directly into the body of UK law. Parliamentary scrutiny committees supervise the process, as does the European Parliament, but their principal task is to sift and report to Parliament.

This inventory shows the advanced state not only of what in general terms we understand by interdependence, but of an inexorable process of integration with our European partners. For the moment, obligations within the Atlantic alliance and the world economic community are more narrowly or loosely defined. Yet they are real, whether we wish to heed their rules or not. Those which bind us to our EC partners, however, are both binding and irreversible. More than that, they are progressive in a commitment both to pursue further integration and an *a priori* undertaking to apply a present and future body of laws to that effect.

Beyond these limitations, poolings and joint exercises of sovereignty there lies the transnational exposure to nuclear energy, both civil and military, and more pedestrian forms of pollution. Clouds of radioactivity from Chernobyl, or acid rain from whoever will admit to it, are equally no respecters of frontiers. A first and immediate problem in Europe will be to deal with the time-bombs of similarly accident-prone reactors and the palls of solids and gases emitted by primeval industries in the East. Yet awaiting us is the future task of coping with the effects of rising living standards of the millions to whom we have held out the promise to become indiscriminate consumers and polluters like us.

All along the line, the moral is the same: people who live in confined spaces must learn to live together. That means not only in peace and by sharing common obligations, but also in respect for their common home.

The risk for us as individuals lies in divided loyalties. Attachment to inborn notions of sovereignty, especially in countries conscious of their strong traditions and fearful of diluting them, may compete with the ideals of a greater unity. Perceptions of the patent realities of the modern world may vie with more ancient roots. An individual may risk being torn between the apparent contradictions of the world in which he was cradled and the world in which he now lives.

The challenge is for us to show that these are false antitheses, to find methods to reconcile one with the other rather than to allow them to persist as opposing polarities. The truth is that all will depend upon the system we choose to house our commonality. Alarmists talk of centralism, of a Euro-broth in which we shall all have to submerge our real identities. No one, least of all the founding fathers of Europe and their descendants, has yet sought to advertise such a folly. Is it conceivable that the Frenchman will sacrifice his language, the Swabian his costume, the Englishman his club in which—come what may by way of European legislation—ladies are allowed to step on to consecrated male ground only at the appropriate hour?

The illuminating truth is that in the new Europe we shall all be minorities, representing and defending our own traditions and language, our customs and diets, our chapels and rites. Like all minorities, the greater the thrust towards integration, the more assertive our individualism. Any system which, whilst offering us the benefits of a common space within common borders, is unable to come to terms with that, will stand no chance of gaining our vote or loyalty—let alone permanence. We may be confident that an appropriate design will emerge from the sheer pressure of necessity. And if it serves us western 'minorities', it should be capable in due course of embracing those to the east as well.

7

Containment of Conflicts

'Civil wars are internationalised by the intervention of outside states.'

HEDLEY BULL

A zone of instability

Minority issues are the legacy of centuries of feuding over European real estate. This has left a zone of instability, extending over most of the countries of eastern Europe so lately roused by a fresh dawn of democracy and self-expression. Old longings, legitimised by the new respect for human rights, have produced a heady mixture.

What, more precisely, are the potential threats they pose to European security? To identify them, we need to trace their roots in 19th century history and in the areas once covered by two great 'Empires'—the Austro-Hungarian and the Ottoman. We must go back to a previous wave of revolution which, with equal force, swept across Europe in 1848. For most of the peoples involved, its aims were fundamentally nationalist.

The Czechs, who for two hundred years had been submerged without identity, began suddenly to demand a separate home made up of Bohemia, Moravia and Silesia. Declaring their complete autonomy, they established a provisional government and parliament in Prague. Support was gained from a Pan-Slav movement, extending over eastern Europe into Russia. Whilst Austria put a swift end to the Czech insurrection, it had to concede Hungarian demands by sanctioning a separate nation.

Within Hungary, however, Croats, Slovenes and Serbs were aspiring to a separate state of southern Slavs to which the Romanians of Transylvania would also have acceded. Decades later, a free Croatia was to become the symbol of the Southern Slav concept of Yugoslavia. Meanwhile a Croatian invasion of Hungary enabled Austria to restore its dominion over the new state, effectively granting the Magyars greater autonomy in consolidating the Empire's rule over the Slavs. Outwardly, the old order had been restored, but below the surface the shock waves were soon to lead to new eruptions.

Elsewhere, in France, Germany and Italy, the revolution gave an impulse for the coalescing of principalities into nation states. Thrones were rocked, frontiers contested, alliances came and went. In time the pieces settled into larger patterns, new rivalries broke out, old states were marginalised or disintegrated. The vigour of the new aspirants led to more and more intense conflicts, and eventually to world war.

Meanwhile the Ottoman Empire, too, had to succumb to history, nationalism and jealousies. The Balkan principalities—Serbia, Montenegro, Greece—were affected by the revolutionary fever but were dealt with promptly by Russian and Turkish troops. However, despite pressures from the great powers supporting continued Ottoman rule, Turkey—the 'sick man of Europe'—was unable to reform. Again encouraged by the Pan-Slavs, the Christians of Bosnia and Herzegovina rose against the Turks in 1875. The Bulgarians, Serbians and Montenegrins joined the revolt. The Congress of Berlin gave Austria rights to Bosnia and Herzegovina, later to be annexed completely to curb the Serbs. It divided Bulgaria into a northern part remaining under full Turkish control, and a southern autonomous zone with a Christian governor. Romania had to cede Bessarabia to the Russians but received Dobruja instead. Other small parcels were redistributed to Montenegro and Greece.

It was not the formula to bring stability. Bulgarians demanded unity and were attacked by the Serbs. Over the remaining years of the century, Greeks went to the aid of Crete and were subdued; Armenians in Turkey revolted and were exterminated; Macedonia, itself riven by racial dissent, demanded liberty and remained one of the Balkans' lasting trouble spots. The 'Young Turks', emigrés exposed to western thought, began to gain allies among their country's Balkan administrators.

The final act for both Empires opened in 1912. Bulgaria entered into alliances with Serbia and Greece and, together with Montenegro, declared war upon Turkey. Surprisingly, their victory was swift; but it was unable to satisfy their own ambitions. The Bulgarians attacked the Serbs, who were joined by the Greeks, Montenegrins and Romanians. An uneasy peace led directly to the fateful shot, fired in Sarajevo but plotted in Belgrade, which assassinated the heir to the Austrian throne and mobilised the armies for the First World War.

It is instructive to dwell for a moment on this continual ebb and flow of nationalist fervour. Through the confusion of warring minorities can be seen the dominant trend of big power ambition and inconstancy in everything other than in suppression, dismemberment and the granting of temporary favours. It was an age in which war and punitive campaigns came to hand as easily as sporting tournaments and glittering galas.

Even more salutary for us today is the recollection of the great Peace Conference held at The Hague in the closing year of the century. Then as now, revulsion at the continual blood-letting had reached a zenith. Hopes of a different future began to be nourished by a growing liberalism. A new phenomenon—public opinion—had to be taken into consideration. Then as now, involvement of the New World was seen as guaranteeing a new philosophy.

Every nation in Europe took part, as did the United States, China and Japan. In addition to outlawing expanding bullets, poison gas and devices dropped from balloons, its crowning achievement was the creation of an international court to oversee the agreement that disputes between states were henceforth to be settled by arbitration. It proclaimed that the end of the century of nationalism was to herald the advent of that of internationalism. But the custom of hedging one's bets with ad hoc alliances—some secret, some overt—was too deeply ingrained. The web of commitments and obligations grew until the cashing of that one cheque in Sarajevo activated the whole unseen enterprise.

Further opportunities to stabilise eastern Europe were lost with the Treaty of Versailles. The new states of Czechoslovakia and Yugoslavia it confirmed owed nothing to the sorry history of the region: both flew in the face of a sensible demographic design. They were a political hotchpotch of different nationalities, religions and allegiances—the one of Czechs, Poles, Ukrainians, Slovaks and Germans, the other of Serbs, Croats, Slovenes, Bosnians and Montenegrins. Millions of Germans, Russians and Ukrainians formed a precarious part of a resurrected Poland, a legacy of its long partitioning between Austria, Germany and Russia. In Hungary—still at war with the Czechs, Romanians and Serbs—the spread of communism was quashed, as elsewhere outside Russia. On the Baltic, Estonia, Latvia and Lithuania had been able to re-establish their independence in the shadow of that revolution.

The post-war world proved to be the age of dictatorship. From the earliest examples in Russia, Turkey, Hungary and Italy, it spread to Poland, Portugal, Yugoslavia, Bulgaria, Greece, the Baltic states, and to Germany, Austria and Spain. Once again, Europe was set on an inevitable—if this time predictable—collision course. Once again, also, the 'zone of instability' to the east was in disarray. Under the threat of German expansion the Little Entente of successor states to the Austro-Hungarian empire—Czechoslovakia, Romania and Yugoslavia—broke up; whilst Poland aimed desperately to face both ways. Hitler seemed free to take what he wished of Czechoslovakia; Poland, too, helped itself to a little bit, before being invaded first by Germany, then by the Soviets—who also took the opportunity to regain the Baltic states.

Post-Second World War events saw the Soviet Union arrange frontiers and governments very much according to its own will. The lands annexed from Poland remained within the USSR, the former being compensated with East Prussian lands beyond the Oder–Neisse line. The communist government in Czechoslovakia ceded Ruthenia to the Soviets. Yugoslavia, Romania, Hungary, Bulgaria and Albania were brought under 'People's Democracies'. When finally the Soviet occupation zone in Germany was also detached from four-power control, Churchill was able to speak grimly of the 'Iron Curtain' which had descended across Europe. Although becoming less impenetrable with time, it was to remain there for more than forty years.

Now that it has lifted, it is no idle digression to have looked at the problems of an area for which, as part of that wider Europe which has once more opened itself to the world, we have to reassume responsibility. What we have inherited is an 'arc of crisis' stretching from the Baltic to the Adriatic and the Black Sea. It behoves us to find a system within which the trail of a century and a half of violence which we have followed can be neutralised, a system to defuse old hatreds and ambitions before they are capable of reaching flashpoint.

To make the task more urgent, it is necessary only to remember that in all this we have not yet turned to look at the similar dangers already besetting the Soviet Union itself. There, in a dozen places, we can see the real drama being played out, our fears of brimming violence already materialised.

On a still wider canvas, we see areas where outside intervention has served to internationalise local conflicts: the civil war in Spain, the post-war harvest of Korea, Vietnam, Cambodia, Angola and so many others. Some were corrupted by the superpowers of their day, others by internal divisions exacerbated by outsiders. The parallels for eastern Europe—where one country's nationhood is its neighbour's ethnic minority—are alarming. Our new all-European security system must be capable of requiting minorities clamouring for reunification, as much as states threatening action in defence of minorities across the border.

Unlike the 19th-century empires which sought to contain and dominate all manner of peoples within themselves, and in the end succeeded only in giving hostages to their rival powers, we need to ensure that all who have a legitimate interest are included in the system. As the Ottoman and Habsburg experience has shown, and the League of Nations confirmed, unless a security zone is total it cannot survive.

But it cannot rely on political pressures alone. One unknown factor in eastern Europe is the decay of national armed forces. They are of at least two distinct types: those dedicated to the Warsaw Pact, and those responsible for internal security. The latter appear mostly to have vanished or to be at pains to give the impression of having turned to innocent civilian pursuits. Yet in Romania they clearly survive as an organised force and their eradication elsewhere may not be—or remain—as complete as it seems.

The more immediate dangers, however, are represented by disaffected or unemployed individuals and units of the armed forces, both national and Soviet forces awaiting demobilisation or withdrawal. There are reports of defections, as well as of friction between occupying—but no longer occupied—garrisons and local populations. Do they constitute loose cannon balls, likely to blunder relatively harmlessly around the scene until eventually absorbed into civilian life? Or are they dum-dums waiting to explode and splinter in unpredictable directions?

Whichever the likely turn of events, an urgent task for the Warsaw Pact as well as for the temporary guardians of European security will be to see that force reductions, as well as the supervision of idle forces on notice of redeployment, are implemented with an eye to maximum security. Any all-European organisation will certainly need to be given the authority to deal with such matters.

The significance of the cultural dimension

We in the West tend to put culture near the bottom of our priorities. For us it is a dimension so subconscious that it is regarded as slightly aberrant even to talk about it. We who have the full ability for self-expression, and abundant access to other cultures we admire, can afford to be like that. For those who lack that ability, culture—*their* culture—has a powerful and symbolic attraction.

For all of us, whether consciously or subconsciously, culture means recognition. We see in it echoes of our past, of the people and places in which we grew up, of the communities in which we belong. More than that, it is the recall to traditions—sometimes age-old—whose flavour and disciplines we absorbed in our early years. Whether the sound of trout-streams or of Bach cantatas, the taste of farm bread or of matzos, the smell of peat or incense—what is evoked is more than nostalgic memories, it is the whole culture of the people whom we recognise as 'us'.

When Goering said the word *Kultur* made him reach for his gun, it was not because he disliked art or theatre or Beethoven. It was precisely because he recognised that culture meant loyalties which he and his party were unable to control. It meant the insidious undermining of totalitarianism through the evocation of folk lore and memories. It is equally dangerous for us today to confuse the dimension of that culture with high-brow pursuits, sectional tastes and elitism.

Yet art is in no way separate from that folk culture. Through the ages, the one has drawn its inspiration from the other. Art itself constitutes a vital part of the process of recognition and bonding. Its importance to endangered communities lies in the fact that it can survive in clandestine conditions. By carrying symbols unknown to an oppressor, it can become the vehicle for opposition and hope. Art is ambiguity, and ambiguity is safe from persecution. It is the ultimate freedom.

Perhaps it is significant that on both occasions when the Russian empires crumbled—the one Tsarist, the other Marxist—it came at the height of the country's cultural esteem. In music, ballet, literature, Russian artists excelled and were received with universal admiration. Both those who came to the West and those who stayed, the Pasternaks and Dostoyevskys, the Nijinskys and the Benes, the Shostakoviches and Mussorgskys, have been fêted and acclaimed, as much for their courage as for the monuments to their creativeness.

The cultural allegiances of the peoples of eastern Europe are a reality with which we need to come to terms. The more they have been denied through the centuries, the stronger the symbolism they have acquired. They are now the focus of nationalist ambitions which need in some way to be canalised and fulfilled. It will be our task to see that they do not remain isolated or repressed. Most of all we need to ensure that they do not become the rallying calls of separatism.

People who live in cultural ghettos not only excite suspicion in those who are excluded. Whether freemasons or Jews, closed rites are considered a threat to those who fail to understand their import. Yet beyond that, such communities can easily punish themselves by excluding themselves from sharing in a wider culture.

Most of us in the West are aware of the pleasures and excitement of discovering other people's customs, participating in the simplicities of Portugese fishermen or the ornate rituals of Orthodox worship. We know that we can do so without sacrificing our own beliefs or being disloyal to our own community.

Thus there is a dual function involved in using culture to heal the divisions within eastern Europe, and especially among the minorities. The more important of the two is to demonstrate that the full cultural offering of the West is at last open to them. That means to ensure access both by bringing it to them, and them to it. It also means showing them that they can find receptive ground for an appreciation of their own culture in a western society avid to learn and taste more of the world's cultures.

The second function is to show that, through access to western cultures, the peoples of eastern Europe can become part of a community which transcends their local problems. Their historical restrictions, the being pinned down between hostile and rapacious neighbours, the feeling of persecution—all these can in time be overcome by making minorities feel part of a wider community whose heritage they are entitled to share.

It should be a voyage of rich discovery for both parties. And the gains, in terms of cultural as well as political security, will make a vital contribution to efforts at last to construct and maintain a European peace.

Building a framework to contain conflict

If collective security can be built only on total participation of all those involved, the 'Helsinki process' already offers a fair beginning. During a period of détente in the Cold War, 35 nations consisting of the whole of Europe—including the Vatican and with the sole exception of Albania—together with the United States, Canada and the Soviet Union signed an agreement whose principal aim was the reduction of tension in Europe. Improbably for the year 1975, it dealt with human rights and even laid down procedures for verification of abuses. Perhaps with hindsight it was the first attempt by the Soviet leadership to regain admittance to the international community. At the time it seemed little more than a successful propaganda coup to impress world opinion, the more so as infringements of human rights and strict control of allegedly liberalised cultural and other contacts persisted. But it also succeeded in setting guidelines for economic co-operation and a security balance.

It nevertheless set in motion an effect which Mr Brezhnev certainly did not intend. To the citizens of the East, the 1975 Act laid an obligation upon their rulers to observe human rights at home. It provided a frame of legitimacy for protest and encouraged scattered opposition groups to become welded into a movement for the recognition of universal human rights. This in turn created a bridge for civil liberties movements to support each other across their own as well as East-West frontiers.

Its signal achievement. however, was to establish the Conference of Security and Co-operation in Europe (CSCE) as a permanent body ensuring periodic contacts and the means of expanding and supervising the process. Immediately after the end of the Cold War, and particularly in face of the prospect of German unification, it proved its capacity to become more than a talking shop to purvey pious platitudes. Real work has already been achieved. The first landmark was the Copenhagen accord of June 1990 on a declaration guaranteeing the rights of citizens and committing governments to introduce and maintain multi-party democracy.

This has since been enshrined as one of the binding commitments in the Charter of Paris signed in November 1990. Others include freedom of movement and the enjoyment of economic, social, cultural and property rights. Its effect is to bind the Soviet Union and the whole of eastern Europe to standards of democracy and human rights which only a short time ago would have been unthinkable. This has in turn had a marked influence on all other contacts and negotiations, which the West has always linked with progress on individual rights and the rule of law.

Significantly, the Charter acknowledges also the rights of minorities. Not only does it extend to them the fundamental freedoms, it seeks to respect their special status and problems. It goes some way towards a commitment on the use by national minorities of their own language in schools as well as in dealings with the authorities, and in recognising the need for exemptions from conscription. It is an early recognition that the S in CSCE is intimately bound up with the minority question.

The Charter has rightly been called a new Magna Carta, guaranteeing fundamental rights to every citizen of the northern hemisphere. Its ratification will add legal force to the principles enunciated in the Copenhagen declaration and enshrine them in national law—and, more importantly, practice. The gap between the establishment of principles and their actual application is one with which the CSCE has been confronted from the beginning. Much has been learnt from the experience of the UN and it is clear that members intend to avoid past mistakes.

For some time past, there already had been general agreement on the need to institutionalise the CSCE, to give it the capacity not only to exist between meetings but to work, to monitor and to take initiatives. The 1990 Washington summit had agreed on the setting up of a permanent secretariat to discharge these functions; this has now been achieved. Many other proposals were advanced for the improvement of the CSCE's functioning, and for endowing it with the capacity to become an effective and binding instrument for political and practical concertation.

Ex-Soviet Foreign Minister, Mr Shevardnadze, was the first to advance the concept of a Greater Europe Council as a supreme European policy making body. It would be based on the CSCE and its secretariat and would formalise its work. Its tasks would be to see that the rules of democracy were being observed in CSCE countries and to monitor military stability. The Council would consist of the 34 heads of government and meet every two years. Its work would be prepared by a committee of their foreign ministers, meeting perhaps twice a year and served by a permanent co-ordinating commission. Such a structure would also encourage the development and co-ordination of proposals for all-European co-operation within a series of CSCE expert committees.

The proposal demonstrates the seriousness with which the Soviet Union came to view the need for permanent consultation, co-ordination and monitoring machinery. In that it was joined by many others: the Polish proposal for a not dissimilar Council of European Co-operation, a European Human Rights Institute, the Belgian Foreign Minister Mark Eyskens' European Security Council and Energy Community, and even President Mitterrand's call for a European Confederation. All recognised the need for an all-European structure within which to tackle jointly the whole complex of inter-related problems facing our continent.

The CSCE and European security

Under the Charter of Paris the CSCE is now developing such an institutional structure: a Council of Ministers as the central forum of political consultation; a Secretariat to service it; and a parliamentary assembly to build links with national parliaments.

In addition to safeguarding the rights of the individual and of minorities, the substance of CSCE co-operation covers a wide range of common concerns. It embraces economic development and transition to a free market, transport, energy, environmental protection, and action against drugs and terrorism. An Office for Free Elections in Warsaw will monitor electoral procedures. Cultural centres in cities of other participating States, and wider exchanges in the arts complete the current agenda for the purposeful cementing of the European peace. Yet there is more at stake.

Countries which place their trust in collective institutions also require some physical safeguards. However flawed the principles of the Warsaw Pact, it did provide a shield for the protection of its members from a notional enemy; and the same is doubly true of NATO. Political protection is fine, until someone unruly takes up arms, even in the face of all reason. Who will then stand guard over a deliberately enfeebled victim, whose defences have been disbanded because everyone had foresworn the use of force? The moral is that any mechanism for the preservation of peace must have the capacity to enforce that peace.

The new Conflict Prevention Centre in Vienna is the instrument for crisis management and reducing the risk of confrontation. Without an enforcement capacity, however, its role can only be preventative. In time it might be strengthened by the addition of machinery for complaints, inspection and verification procedures. Yet the question has been raised whether it is realistic to expect CSCE to include such sophisticated mechanisms without the risk of overloading it. Perhaps it would be useful here to distinguish between the various functions involved, i.e. between monitoring and verification of arms reduction agreements, conciliation procedures, and the actual peace-keeping through sanctions and the ultimate use of force.

In order to come to grips with monitoring and verification, the first step will be to build on those things which are already in place and have shown that they can work harmoniously. A good example is the Stockholm agreement on notification of major military exercises. This has now been improved through the presence of observers from 'the other side' and become a part of the confidence-building process. It could even be that, between now and their withdrawal in 1994, Soviet units stationed in East Germany will be invited to take part in German military maneouvres.

A second step could easily be taken with the adoption of the NATO-type annual review process. This is the 'soft directive process' in which each country explains its policy implementation, its force levels and their dispositions. Whilst this has been used in the past to monitor defence expenditures and the agreed build-up of NATO forces, the process as such would lend itself equally to the logging of force reductions. Such a review forum can be readily linked on the one hand with the ongoing negotiations on conventional and nuclear arms and, on the other, to physical verification procedures which are already in process of development.

These mechanisms will before long develop a dual role. Although created as part of the negotiating process between the two blocs, they will be capable at the same time of being transferred to serve the CSCE for its own monitoring and verification needs. They have a definite place in the Conflict Prevention Centre's annual exchange of military information. We are therefore already seeing the outlines of an emerging Europe-wide system.

Conciliation procedures will present a more complex field. The essence of recent bloc and superpower bargaining has been that no conflict or irreconcilable difference of view would emerge to hinder the process. The reason is simple, for there was no forum or machinery for conciliation. The parties themselves were locked in the negotiations, and it was their responsibility to find solutions. Until there are effective institutions that may yet hold its dangers, for success still hangs entirely on continuation of the present climate of goodwill and resolve to find agreement, come what may.

Both sides are therefore anxious to build up a system within which conciliation will become physically possible. Both see it as a step which is vital for the achievement of more permanent security. Hence both now look anxiously to the CSCE and its Conflict Prevention Centre as the nearest available raft.

Conciliation is the process of voluntarily submitting oneself and one's disputes to as independent a forum as one can find. It therefore presupposes some third parties whose opinions and arbitration both sides to the dispute will be able to respect and honour. The 34-member CSCE holds out precisely that quality. The more it can be institutionalised and fitted out with prestigious organs, the easier will it be for powerful nations to accept its jurisdiction. In the case of conciliation, therefore, a new road has yet to be travelled; and the process will be the same for the superpowers as for the rest of the CSCE's members.

Much the same must be true of the putting in place of the actual peace-keeping mechanism. By definition, it is an instrument to be brought into play only once all attempts at conciliation have proved abortive. In a collective rather than in a national sense, it is therefore the 'continuation of policy by other means.' As such, it must be a part of the same institutional forum, brought into play by the same authority.

We can see that the responsibilities to be placed upon CSCE have been described in ascending order, from the simplest to the most onerous. Whilst it can take over procedures for monitoring and verification ready-made, conciliation will require an afflux of authority to which proud nations can credibly bow their knee and, in effect, surrender a part of their sovereignty. The seal would be set upon that surrender if compliance then becomes mandatory through the potential application of sanctions or force. At the same time, those required to commit units to a multinational peace-keeping force will be incurring future risks—in terms of lives and political imbroglios—which could become as difficult to defend at home as in the field.

What will the establishment of such an authority demand? Can it be a compact, functional operation such as Euratom, the EC's atomic energy control community or its international equivalent? Or does it require the full panoply of an international organisation such as the United Nations, with assemblies, councils, specialised agencies, uncounted committees and field staff? What in essence would be the source of its authority, and how would it be governed and administered?

Attempts have already been made to answer some of these questions. Among a rich variety of analyses, a common factor is an examination of the extent to which existing fora may be capable of providing the base. Essentially these would be a grouping of the 22 current members of NATO and the Warsaw Pact; the expansion of NATO, as proposed by the Hungarian foreign minister; a 'European solution' based on the EC and/or Western European Union (WEU), or on a CSCE minus the superpowers; and a totally CSCE-based formula with the gradual addition of countries which might gain independence from the Soviet Union.

The most detailed review of these possibilities is made in a paper presented to the European Parliament's sub-committee on security and disarmament by Michael Palmer.[7] It lists at least eight possible models for a European security structure. One possibility clearly is a simple association between NATO and the Warsaw Pact, quickly discarded because of the perpetuation of the bloc system, not to mention the atrophy of one of the constituents.

More viable models would all have in common the individual adherence of all the countries embraced in the two alliances, with neutral or non-aligned CSCE members also having the option to join. The differences would be represented by the presence of a European core, whether based on the existing Western European Union, a European Defence Community growing up alongside the EC, or on the EC itself; and by the actual methods of who joins what.

Also defined is a crisis management system developing over time. It could begin with present forms of co-operation, evolving into a longer term all-European security system associating the United States and the USSR, or alternatively the CSCE institutions together with a mechanism for the peaceful settlement of disputes. A final building block would be an all-European arms control agency.

The chairman of the same sub-committee, Hans-Gert Pöttering MEP,[8] has proposed a European security union, modelled closely on the paragon of NATO as a supremely successful example for 'the peaceful co-existence of former arch-enemies such as Germany and France'. The plan foresees reducing all national forces to a minimum complement of professional armies, integrated amongst themselves to the extent that, within a short time, war between them would have become impossible.

The fundamental question confronting all such architectural attempts is whether to create new institutions or adapt existing ones. Is it a task for bold new designs, or a gradualist evolution co-ordinating what is already functioning? The CSCE has certainly proved itself to be one of those, and its major advantage lies in having precisely the necessary membership. It does not raise questions of whether belonging to it can be reconciled with neutrality: the neutrals are already a part of it. Even a peace-keeping role would be fully in accord with their principles. There would be no difficulty either in giving it the full status of a regional organisation as envisaged in the UN Charter.

The main question then to be resolved is how to get there. What do we use as building blocks, and how do we bridge the uncomfortable gap during which all of us are exposed and anything can still happen?

From a bipolar to a tripolar relationship?

A nightmarish risk during that transition is that, whilst the Soviet Union is preoccupied with pressing internal problems within its fracturing union, a situation could arise in eastern Europe which demands some kind of peace-keeping intervention. Clearly the CSCE would be the forum to decide upon the action; but is it realistic to think that NATO or US forces would be asked to participate? More likely is that the appeal would be made to the EC as the western European political forum.

Is there a role for a European guarantor? One of the impulses for the 1989 Revolution was that all eyes were focused on the EC, its prosperity and its liberties. Since then it has proved itself ready to share those privileges with the newly democratic countries and maintained its reputation for political impartiality and fair dealing. Most of eastern Europe is ready for some kind of association as a prelude to full membership.

This is only one of the many questions about security which will from now on be asked with increasing frequency and insistence of the EC. It is the result of its standing throughout Europe as much as of its internal political co-operation, let alone the projected political union. Is it not necessary to complete the EC's political, economic and social responsibilities with a fourth dimension, that of security? Is it possible for it to go on not being able to take cognisance of security matters?

There can be many answers to this question, but perhaps the most plausible is a 'Yes . . . but'. Certainly the time has come when security questions have to be placed squarely on the EC's agenda. Concrete proposals for merging WEU with the Community were advanced during the Italian Presidency of it. It is already involved in matters affecting defence industries, economic security and political responses to foreign policy issues. However, that is far from implying that the EC should now acquire competence for defence matters. The Gulf crisis showed that its major contribution is to provide political co-ordination. The actual military response it wisely left to NATO, the UN and bilateral parleys involving the US as the leader of the western action.

The most difficult thing for an assembly of states is to agree on the use of lethal force. The EC knows this, and the CSCE will not take long to find out. It is at least one reason why the EC is rightly reluctant to become involved in such decisions. Another is the position of France on matters on the borderline between defence and foreign policy. Rightly or wrongly, France is intent on maintaining its independence of action across most of this area. It has withdrawn from the military command of NATO and has taken an individual stance on most—but by no means all—occasions involving the composition of a multinational force.

French official opinion holds that it is an advantage of the EC that its members are able to give a variety of responses according to the needs of each case, and the interests of the members involved. This may be an elegant way to retain one's own independence of action whilst benefiting from membership of a powerful club. Yet there are instances where the ambiguity created has had positive results. It is well known that in international crises, as in hijackings, the art has become first to keep talking, second to have impeccable sources of up-to-date intelligence, third to maintain political control over the military options, fourth to allow pauses for reflection, and finally to take the adversary into one's confidence, allowing him to follow what is happening to him. The same process can be productive, so long as it is played out as part of a firm front.

Though the UK is a more stalwart ally in military matters, the French position is remarkably close to the official British view of the EC. Is there a possibility of discovering more common ground, especially on defence matters? Is it possible that a reduction in the US military presence in Europe could lead to a more positive French role, even if it does not re-enlist fully in NATO?

The question of a European pillar within NATO must needs acquire additional urgency as budgetary pressures and mutual force reductions take effect. It is barely conceivable that the EC's NATO members should fail to rise to the opportunity, the more so as Germany's position will demand a high degree of concertation. Whether it distances itself from the NATO fold, for instance by becoming disinclined to host nuclear weapons or foreign troops, or whether it assumes a naturally dominant role within Europe, it is essential for it to act in concert with its European allies.

There is, of course, another candidate organisation on which to repose the European pillar: WEU. To the extent that it groups almost all the EC's NATO members (including France), is a specifically military organisation, and has well-defined control and policy functions, it is perhaps a more logical choice as carrier of the European defence function. In *A Step beyond Fear*,[9] Christopher Layton has set out how this could work effectively by placing NATO's European activities under the WEU wing. WEU could, for instance, provide a home and a permanent secretariat for NATO's Eurogroup and the Independent European Programme Group (IEPG). WEU's Standing Armaments Committee could then be merged into IEPG. France might find this a convenient way to become associated with Eurogroup and establishing a closer, though still not integral, link with NATO.

This will not absolve the EC from concerning itself with security matters; indeed, to follow the logic of recent events, it should be the political master of WEU. It would lead to the same procedures as were developed during the Iraq crisis: the EC taking the political decisions and co-ordinating the diplomatic moves; and WEU concerting European military moves in readiness for deliberations of the Atlantic Council.

Such an ordering would be as healthy for NATO as for the Europeans. In addition, it would facilitate first the process of political union, since neither neutrality nor an independent view of defence matters would be a bar; and secondly the eventual accession of east European states.

A tripolar relationship in European affairs offers a structure seemingly best suited to the logic of present and foreseeable circumstances. Both superpowers are essential to the European peace process. Each one is needed to balance the other and so that former opponents may subsume their differences in co-operation. That, however, leaves Europe itself in a somewhat supine position and in danger of becoming a passive spectator in its own fate. That could just be acceptable if all decisions were subordinated to the CSCE, in whose councils the Europeans would have at least a numerical majority. Yet it ignores a substantial part of the equation—Germany.

A strong and active EC is, as has been argued elsewhere, a *sine qua non* of German unification. That is Germany's own desire and it should be that of every one of its neighbours and allies. Germany's weight is too great for it not to be firmly entrenched within a strong organisational structure, to which it can add enormous importance and prestige. Both its economy and its political power are best integrated within an ever more closely knit European union. Yet that will not succeed unless that union is ready to play its role in world affairs as Germany alone might in future be ready to do. It is therefore the destiny of the EC to continue apace the logic of its integration, and, however reluctantly, to become a world power.

EC members will still have a full menu of choices as to the form they prefer that integration to take. But the process itself is ineluctible.

That being so, the tripolar relationship is also not so much a matter of choice as of reality. Its beginnings can already be seen: the US has begun the practice of discussions with the EC in parallel to those within NATO; and the Soviet Union accorded it full recognition as a prelude to allowing eastern Europe to choose its own destiny. Both want to talk only with a coherent body composed of those who are capable of exercising power.

The EC has a further mission. As a manifestly successful example of regional integration it should make its own contribution to the design of CSCE institutions. What has been achieved within the EC by way of reconciliation, of economic progress and of aligning political objectives is precisely what the whole of Europe now needs. A CSCE made in the EC's image could be the West's major gift to the new democracies to the east. As their own unhappy structure disintegrates, it can provide them with a new one within which to find greater tolerance and fulfilment.

Other existing institutions such as the Council of Europe will have important roles to play. The Council has traditionally looked to increase links with eastern Europe and full membership will be a natural first step to integrate the new democracies with western Europe. It will bring them into western councils and prepare them for future membership of the EC.

As the CSCE institution-building process develops, there will be other ways of implanting the fruits of western Europe's hard-won experience. In overall terms, the EC should be able to provide to eastern Europe the same assurances as the US did to the West after 1946. Only the Europeans' own bungling could now deny them the opportunity at last to build a zone of stability.

8

Wanted—New Forms of
Statecraft

'To look for a continuation of harmony between a number of independent,
unconnected sovereignties in the same neighbourhood, would be to disregard
the uniform course of human events, and to set at defiance the accumulated
experience of ages.'

ALEXANDER HAMILTON

The transnational age

Just as in the 19th century fiefdoms and principalities coalesced into
nation-states, so in the 20th century these states are growing together
into still larger units. For the time being, the term 'supranational' has
described their relations and the sharing of functions between them.
No clear concept has as yet evolved of a recognisable entity which
surpasses the nation-state.

When we speak of regional co-operation, we are describing merely
the process by which states the world over have begun to tend their
common interests. We are not even defining the many different forms
of association which are possible, let alone their intensity. Yet it is
significant that, however varied its forms, the same process is at work
in virtually every continent.

Our own European Community is already one of the most
advanced examples of a post-war generation of such regional bodies.
In the Americas, the Andean Pact and the Caribbean Community, in
Asia the Association of South-East Asian Nations, the Economic
Community of West African States and the Southern Africa Development Co-operation Conference are only a few of those which are today
shaping the development of our globe. All these have quite specific

tasks for economic and political co-operation. There are many more, such as the Council of Europe and the regional bodies of the United Nations, whose aims are to co-ordinate, rather than integrate, their members' activities across a broader spectrum.

Yet the hallmark of our age is not the notion of regional co-operation but its adoption throughout a world progressively required to confront a similar set of problems. Whether through their own economic development or that of their neighbours, developing countries are forced to adhere to international standards and conventions which lie outside their experience, or to advance to more sophisticated practices in which their size and location place them at a disadvantage. The debt crisis alone illustrates the problem—its causes born of inexperience, its penal effects inescapable because the only way out is through an international economic system whose activating levers lie beyond the debtor's reach.

The gathering of states which recognise their own impotence and the opportunities offered by joining with others goes back to the alliances of antiquity. The trend persists through the Holy Roman Empire and the improbable 'federation' of 350 German states which was the product of the Thirty Years' War (1618–48). But a step of quite a different order was taken in 1781 when the Thirteen States of America established a central government under the Articles of Confederation—the first modern example of independent states voluntarily submitting to a common government. Since then we have witnessed similar developments in Australia, in Canada, India and Nigeria.

Significantly, all were former British dominions or possessions. Indeed, in the dissolution of Empire it seemed to become a favoured formula to bring together, within a federation, territories patently unable to form a more viable economic or political unit. Some attempts where internal inequalities proved too great to endure are those in the West Indies, and in Central and East Africa. A rather more successful post-war example, whose design also owes something to British political thought, is the German Federal Republic (FRG).

Not all have had an unchequered passage. The American civil war, the Biafran campaign in Nigeria, the current constitutional crisis in Canada, are challenges to be resolved when the ambitions of a constituent state begin to run counter to the will of the majority. It can mean that there is something wrong with the form of constitution, or— —as with slavery and the Biafrans' dynamism—that an economic interest opposes itself to the common goal. The history of the Swiss

Confederation throughout three centuries of religious tensions, economic inequalities and domination from outside its borders provides a full inventory of what adaptations may be necessary. Yet most of its convulsions have mirrored the social, religious and constitutional events which beset all states, whether unitary or federal, and which not even the United Kingdom failed to escape.

There is a widely held belief that such political agglomerations must needs develop into great monoliths. A glance even at the United States shows that this belongs to the realm of myths. Despite the Coca-Cola culture and the imprint of other ubiquitous products, differences between states have remained so marked, their ability to govern their own affairs and set taxes, look after their own social problems and security so varied, that it is often hard to believe their ability to agree on crucial issues. Indeed, Washington politics not infrequently reflects the hard bargaining needed to reach consensus.

There is an even wider difference between the ways in which supranational entities have chosen to order their affairs. From the unitary model by which the United Kingdom dominates its four constituent parts, to the confederal pattern of Switzerland and the federal one of the United States and Canada. But these adjectives hide further substantial variations in powers and competences reserved to each State, as well as those exercised centrally. In every case, the balance has been determined first by local factors, then moulded by history and experience. The Philadelphia constitution makers and the founding fathers of the Treaty of Rome were grappling with different problems and had to find different solutions.

In Europe we have developed the Community method. Some believe that there has already been a significant transfer of power. But so long as the Council of Ministers, its members appointed by each government, retains the right to block the Commission's proposals, no fundamental power can be said to have passed. It is precisely because we have recognised the weaknesses of this system that we are now engaged in the debate on how to improve the EC's structure and functioning. Some aspects of sovereignty, as we have seen, have been transferred to be jointly exercised—detached as much by history as by any conscious act. But powers are a different matter; their transfer will require a more purposeful approach.

The challenge for us today, both at home and in the wider world, is to work with, rather than against, the trend towards supranational groupings, for only in that way can we hope to master the diversity of problems which confront us. We have already analysed the instability of our world and the threats it could pose for us. Instead of fearing changes over which we can exercise control, we should beware of those which still lie beyond our writ.

A Europe of the regions

A singular feature of the approaching single European market has been the by-passing of traditional modes of contact. Commercial interests have for long chosen their own routes. But suddenly local authorities and regional governments throughout the EC have discovered their affinities. Officials in Bavaria have realised that some of their problems bear more resemblance to those of Scotland than of neighbouring Baden-Württemberg. From tourism to hill-farming, from public procurement to environmental protection, co-operation between them is blossoming.

The impetus has clearly been the extension of Community policies to such fields, coupled with the opening up of markets and competition to all EC countries. But the response has been immediate, and direct. No one thinks of passing via London or Bonn. Some, like lawyers from southern England setting up offices in northern France, follow their clients. Others buy up companies to gain their foothold. Towns have twinned themselves for decades. Now we are seeing communities or regions growing out of a community of interests.

What is the likely import? First, a wholesome return to the spirit when Europe once before was open to the medieval scholar or trader, when borders served to collect tribute rather than deter people, and the only barriers encountered were wars or pestilence. Freedom of movement as part of life, not just for the grand tour or the annual holiday, is an inestimable right we can now rediscover. Physical frontiers also set limits within the mind. Secondly, our own perceptions of democracy will be strengthened once we gain a better perspective of the real functions of our governments. For too long we have relied on government as the great intermediary in our affairs with the outside world. If we find we can travel, live and work as we please without it, those whose slogan is 'Less government' should be the first to congratulate us.

The concept of a Europe of the regions becomes more significant still as we look East. Perhaps for us citizens of the Community, those freedoms are only a small step beyond what we already take for granted. For east Europeans they open a totally new dimension. Here too the regions have begun to reach out. First were the contacts between those within the two Germanies. Today there are almost as many such links being forged in other countries to the east as on the commercial level. Towns help other towns, regional authorities their counterparts wherever they find common ground. The same applies between east European countries themselves, as much as between East and West.

Some did not wait for the thaw or the Revolution. For the past ten years there has been an active collaboration among the border regions of Friuli in Italy, Carinthia in Austria and Yugoslav Slovenia. In time, they were joined by Bavaria, Styria, Croatia, Venice, Lombardy, the Alto Adige, and finally four Hungarian Komitate. The governments concerned have now taken up the idea and, as the 'Pentagonale', are trying to make it into a formal Danube-Adria co-operation zone. Competences for practical matters have been parcelled out: environmental action to Austria, transport and communications to Italy, small and medium-sized industry to Hungary, telecommunications to Yugoslavia, and cultural affairs to Czechoslovakia. But already Poland, Romania and Bulgaria are knocking on the door, and out of the whole enterprise could grow a new 'Little Entente'.

For countries which are suffering a natural revulsion against centralism, this is clearly the happiest road to take. Avid as they are to learn, to follow decades of hectoring from Moscow with official tutoring by the West would be intolerable. The most that governments can do—and some are doing with great foresight—is to provide the means for such contacts at local official and private level.

There is indeed much to do. Eastern Europe is embarked on two great voyages of rediscovery: democracy and the introduction of a free market system. Democracy is not just a question of national ballots to elect a parliament which will legislate the transition. Democracy has to work at local level, right down to the parish pump, if people are to become involved in the process and develop faith in it. Casting a national vote which someone would actually count was a moment of glory; but having to wait four years for the next chance will not buy loyalty to the new system.

Local and regional authorities throughout the EC have much to contribute. So have party organisations, and those like the Hansard and Electoral Reform societies skilled in building mechanisms to ensure fair play. Exchanges at this level to observe good practice at first hand can make a material difference to the outlook of whole communities.

Much the same holds true for assistance with the intricacies of the free market system. Here the pace must, of course, be determined by each government. The unravelling of property holdings, usually between party and state, is a repellent business which is not for outsiders. Neither is consultation in drafting new legislation on private ownership. Yet this is where local private interests should ensure that they have a say, and experience from other countries can help them to formulate their views.

Out of such beginnings can grow chambers of commerce, business-men's clubs, trade associations and all the other fabric of organisa-tions which group commercial interests. In the new democracies these will be as much for learning the opportunities and techniques of private business as for representing them officially. Here again, not only national private sector bodies but also regional ones have an opportunity to be involved. As within the EC, particular regions will recognise their interests in commercial links, whether within the same neighbourhood or because of structural similarities.

Experiments with democracy and the market system in the East, and with the Community method in the West, form a constellation of circumstances which can itself make for a common bond. Both in fact are liberating movements from the power of the state. Both favour private initiative and the organisations which it has created, rather than the formal creatures on the fringes of government. Both aim to devolve responsibility to the lowest level. They have a great need of each other. It is an hour when fruitful alliances are to be forged between the regions of Europe and the institutions they have built for themselves.

To be sure, other forms of support are necessary. The EC needs to smooth the way by removing trade restrictions, promoting interna-tional action on public debt, and pump-priming the market process with aids to new investment. Like its constituent governments, the EC has an initiating and support function. But its role is the more import-ant, since it can more easily prompt parallel action by the US and Japan.

A vital aspect of the Europe of the regions is, of course, the scope for contacts and action that it gives to areas which might well have no voice in the official relations entertained by their governments. Minority regions will find opportunities to enter into relationships with populations of other countries more sympathetic to their culture and desires for recognition. Clearly, there will need to be safeguards on both sides: against denial of this freedom by their government, and against outside support for political agitation. Both will fall under the CSCE declaration which should ensure a remedy.

Minorities in Bulgaria or Bielorussia may well team up with Bretons or Basques who feel equally marginalised. Already a newly united Berlin has offered to twin with Belfast, the last divided city in Europe. Out of such sympathies can come a clearer understanding of the role and opportunities for sub-national entities, be they regions or minorities. The realisation that they, too, can play a full part in the new Europe can be a healing process. It may defuse precisely those problems which arise from people driven in upon themselves.

A new vitality

Insistence on the need for aid and support for the peoples of the east should not lead us to believe that they have been left impotent and exhausted. The 1989 Revolution was itself a demonstration of their accumulated resources of courage and vitality. Since then there has been a flowering of spirit and hopes. Some, admittedly, have remained stunned by the events, or lost in a world suddenly so alien. Others, as in Romania, are still waiting for full liberation. But everywhere there are people savouring their new freedoms and anticipating the more ponderous actions of governments.

Even in the Soviet Union, infected with scepticism about the reality of economic reforms, there has been a sudden release of intellectual vigour. *Glasnost*, the lifting of censorship, the abandonment of officially imposed artistic standards, above all the process of liberation itself, have everywhere brought creative debate and action. A new interaction with western thought, for long followed from afar, has led to a more honest examination of all forms of endeavour.

The freeing of the resources of the human spirit has been one of the greatest gifts of the Revolution. Although most easily recognised, and romanticised, in the field of art, it is increasingly evident in other fields. Craftsmen, artisans, contractors, entrepreneurs, farmers with precious commodities to sell, have come out of the trenches and are laying the foundations of the private enterprise economy. Government actions can retard, but no longer inhibit their independence. The individual is asserting his freedom to act in his own way within society.

Universities and research bodies are beginning to build on their ability for free exchanges. Although never fully cut off from their western counterparts, the disciplines imposed on them were severe.

Often precisely those with the most open minds were excluded from the system. Among scientists and researchers, cross-fertilisation with ideas and information is producing new inspiration. Removal of the official incubus from university teaching will soon spread a new awareness of liberal concepts and approaches. As in other societies, translation of the benefits into political and economic life will be swift.

It should not be expected that the results will be identical to those in the West. Differing starting points, the pain of oppression, the problems of transition from one system to another, are bound to result in different conclusions. The experience by which they are modified may be alien to ours, yet it is also intensely relevant. We too need to chart a way of overcoming problems in our society. They may be those arising from an excess of freedom rather than repression, yet one is the obverse of the other. Concepts and practices developing in the East will therefore bear as potently on ours in the West as ours will influence theirs.

This mutuality should before long produce some healthy competition. In our comfortable mood of self-congratulation we may take it for granted that our long-cherished ideas will prevail. But we may as easily find ourselves overtaken, ironically by those who have long cherished our ideals from afar. Even if those ideals were potent enough to provide the impetus for revolution, they will inevitably be modifed by others. As in Darwinian evolution, stronger mutations are bound to develop. Societies must learn from each other, but those with the greater vitality will outpace the rest.

Already with Peter the Great, then with 19th-century Japan, we have seen that others are adept at learning western technology. By adopting just that much of the western way of life as is inseparable from its technology, they are capable of injecting their own dynamism, sometimes to rival and surpass what we have been able to achieve with our own tools.

Problems of integration and disintegration

A snapshot of the new Europe presents us with one wing pursuing its process of integration, another in apparent dissolution, and in between an area in transition. For the time being, the future shape and stability of the central zone remain uncertain, since it is not clear to what extent it will respond to the centripetal or centrifugal forces of its neighbours, or to those of nationalism.

Within the EC, accelerated 'deepening' of the process of integration

is in part the consequence of events in the East—through the unification of Germany—as well as the prelude to eventual membership of
the new democracies. The inter-governmental conferences on economic and monetary union, followed by political union, would in other
circumstances not have acquired such impetus, nor their work such
urgency. It has become vital that decisions are not delayed, even if in
the first instance they produce clarification of objectives rather than
action.

Decisions will not be made or implemented without much anguish.
There are fundamental conceptual differences between integrationists
and free traders. Genuine divisions also exist between those wanting
to go further and faster, and those facing difficulties in keeping pace.
The UK economy, for instance, is more prone to inflation, and vulnerable to exchange rate fluctuations, than those of its competitors.
Others, like the three Benelux countries, have already linked themselves to the EC's dominant currency, the deutschmark. There is a
real prospect of a 'two-speed Europe', which could mean that different
levels of prosperity become entrenched.

There are divergences on the meaning and extent of political union.
A common foreign policy will patently carry more weight than twelve
unco-ordinated admonitions. The Iraq crisis has proved how vital a
quick consensus and riposte can be. Yet France may still want to
modulate its responses on, for instance, North African and Pacific
affairs. Germany, too, may in future define policies in relations with
the Soviet Union which have more in common with the Stavropol
agreement on German unification—hammered out bilaterally
between Chancellor Kohl and Mr Gorbachev—than with Community membership. Is it more vital to harmonise views, and particularly actions, or to preserve the ability to speak with many voices?

Under the surface there are recurrent problems about relations
with the USA. Historically the United Kingdom, now Germany, has
laid claim to a special relationship. France has led those who regarded
such Anglo-Saxon bonds with grave suspicion, and as unfitting for a
united Europe. This, at least, is one inferiority complex which should
disappear with the EC's more powerful position in world affairs. But
great care and diplomacy is needed to ensure that the USA itself does
not feel the rupture of a special relationship with Europe.

The nuts and bolts of integration are capable of producing their
own frictions. The ever widening remit of competition policy,
attempts to translate it into an all-embracing codex of social policies,
the remnants of the common agricultural policy—in danger of taking

away from Europe's dwindling but still powerful farming communities what it once so liberally gave them—all these excite as much opposition as support. Soon environmental policies will also begin to bite.

Such are the inevitable difficulties of a diversity of peoples, states and systems growing together. From time to time they appear so formidable as to threaten the whole enterprise. Yet in the final analysis, we can be sure that no one would put up with them if they did not tacitly acknowlege that the game is worth the candle, the prize so great as to merit the sacrifice.

Disintegration of a great empire such as the USSR is in itself a tragic process. Seemingly the absolute reverse of what is at work in the EC, it may on closer examination have more than a few features in common.

Of the 15 republics composing the Soviet Union, most have already declared their independence or sovereignty. All have refused to follow the central government's decree to disarm their militias. One of them, Boris Yeltsin's Russian Federation, contains more than half the population of the USSR in fifteen 'autonomous republics' as well as six 'autonomous regions', occupying a territory twice that of the USA. Further calls for independence have come from within that.

The three Baltic republics continue to challenge Soviet laws, setting their own new code above them. They have refused to send conscripts into the Soviet army and have demanded the return of their soldiers serving in it. The Ukraine has similarly vetoed the deployment of its soldiers outside its territory. These and others of the republics have announced their right to amend their judicial and constitutional status, and to establish their own external relations with third countries. Some, including the Russian Federation, have decided to block exports of strategic commodities to the rest of the USSR.

The nationalism of the real Russia, represented by Mr Yeltsin's core Federation, is deeply ingrained. It harks back to the fierce debates between 19th-century westernisers and traditionalist slavophiles. Now it has become directed against the outer republics of the USSR. There are demands to make the army 'Russian' and to cease training 'our enemies'; and to end the Union structure which allows outsiders to 'exploit' Russian food, oil and metals.

The Kremlin's responses to these challenges betray the weakness of the central government. Having attempted to seek parliamentary endorsement of its own draft treaty for a new form of institutional union, it then outflanked it by taking a referendum direct to the people. Whilst devolving a degree of political power, the draft reserved to the union government eight responsibilities including defence and security, and foreign and monetary policy. The debate will certainly not subsume the ambitions of the republics, for some of them have already arrogated such competences to themselves.

Fighting over ethnic and religious issues also continues sporadically between old enemies, Armenians and Azeris, as well as Georgians. In the end the army has had to be brought in to quell escalating violence.

A further division on the political horizon is the spread of Islam throughout Soviet Central Asia. From Azerbaijan to Uzbekistan, people are turning their faces from Moscow to Mecca. Given leave to follow their religion, but still beset by poverty and hunger, they have enthusiastically embraced the Muslim movement. So far there is little evidence of militantism or fundamentalism, though here and there skirmishes have broken out. There is talk of a Muslim military organisation covering the whole zone, but little evidence of its strength. Yet before long more than half the population of the present USSR is expected to be Muslim.

It represents an added challenge to the conundrum facing the Soviet leadership of how to hold together the more than one hundred nationalities composing the present Soviet Union. There are two possibilities for its resolution. One is quite clearly the threat of anarchy, ethnic conflicts and civil war, which many Soviets increasingly fear. All the material for these is there in abundance, as well as the torches which can set light to the tinder. Regrettably, so also are the arms, including nuclear weapons over which central control could be lost. With republics building up their own militias, and reserving their own men for internal service, any conflict could have the most serious consequences.

A more hopeful scenario would be a consensus on Mr Gorbachev's concept of a flexible union, a 'variable geometry union'. This is not dissimilar from Jean Monnet's erstwhile recipe for a Community offering 'federalism à la carte', enabling the slowest to join with the fastest in a commitment at least to some common tasks. It is a concept which stands somewhere between the firm embrace of a community akin to the EC and a loose grouping like the Commonwealth.

A 'red Commonwealth' might offer the same advantages as that which has grown around Britain, the bringing together of as many peoples as inhabit the USSR, with all their diversities, by applying the minimum of rules. Not even pluralist democracy is one of them, yet 48 independent countries are from time to time able to adopt common measures in uncontentious fields like education, and even subscribe to declarations of sublime principle. Yet it is doubtful that anything as loose—traditionally defined not by what it is, but by what it is not— would meet the Soviet case, where self-determination rather than full independence is the real aspiration.

The main imperative seems to be to remove the imperial relationship and replace it with a more equitable structure, especially in economic relations. But western Europe must be able to offer them an alternative concept, and even help to design a new structure into which they can fit more easily.

A Ukrainian leader visiting London was asked how he saw his republic's 'independence'. 'Not like the USSR,' he said, 'more like the European Community.' It was not just its prosperity which acted as a magnet for eastern Europe, but rather the ideal of democracy in the member states and its extension to relations between them on the Community plane. That ideal may still represent one of the few sweeteners on the eastern Europeans' hard road towards capitalism.

Bizarre as it seems, there is more than a passing similarity between the problems involved in the disintegration of the Soviet Union and those in the integration of the EC. Both are a search for a formula which is more than separatism and less than a centralised state. Undoubtedly the outcomes will be different, since each such grouping is essentially shaped by its members, their relative economic power and the extent of their differences or similarities. In the end what matters is the acknowledgement of a sufficient interest in making common institutions work.

If these are indeed shared problems, there will be common ground between the Soviet Union and the EC and its members. We should not let the opportunity pass to provide what common counsel and study we can, both to the Kremlin and to its rebellious constituents who are able for the first time to test their own ideas against the experience of others.

There are those in the Soviet Union who say, 'Now we have lost the Second World War.' We need urgently to give them the feeling of belonging to the West and of seeing their imagined losses as a common gain.

Still wanted—new forms of statecraft

We began by noting that there was as yet no recognisable paradigm for a political entity which surpasses the nation state. We have seen the already rich variety of supranational associations, yet we are no nearer to a definition.

Perhaps this is not so serious as it seems. Labels, slogans and facile images are not the stuff of objective debate. They have for long bedevilled serious discussion and a meeting of minds on European integration, since they allow little margin for an understanding of the underlying concepts involved. Indeed, were we to copy the models of the past, we would undoubtedly make ourselves hostage to the same fate.

What is wanted today is a simple understanding of the historical processes at work which are propelling us—west Europeans, Soviets, and all those in between and beyond—in similar directions. Being subject to the same compulsion, however, does not absolve us from the responsibility of tracing with care the particular road that we need to travel, and of designing a vehicle which will accommodate all those with whom we intend to embark. Unless each one can be found a comfortable enough seat he will not stand the rigours of the journey and be forever clamouring to step down.

Professor Alting von Geusau has explained it thus, 'Pluralist democracy is neither utopia nor ideology. It is the continuous search for methods to control power by countervailing power, and so restraining the abuse of power over man. It is in our power to extend that search to the future of Europe as a whole.'[10]

What we want is not an abstract definition. We stand in need of the imagination to design a variety of such international vehicles for the urgent purposes of today and those that lie ahead. They should equate to new forms of statecraft, designed to respect the needs of individual peoples as much as those of the countries participating in the enterprise.

The cardinal aim of that modern statecraft must be to put people first. It must create a larger space within which the energies and genius of nations and minorities can properly flourish. With luck and foresight, by attending to them we shall also be ensuring our collective security.

9

A New Strategy

'The military tend to concentrate on capability. The politicians should concentrate on intentions.'

DENIS HEALEY

The requirements

Any new strategy to see us safely through the exciting but still perilous times ahead must do three things: it must satisfy our needs, whatever they are likely to be; it must also satisfy the other side, whoever they are likely to be; and it must take account both of present realities and of future contingencies. That implies weaving an intricate plot, which must allow for several alternative endings. It also demands simultaneous action in a number of directions to ensure that the characters remain under the author's control.

For almost the first time in our history, we do not face a major continental adversary. We therefore have the unique opportunity to try to establish our security in open concert with all other members of our continent. As *The Times* has it, 'If Europe's most virulent disease is the repetition of history, all of Europe must search for a cure.'

Common security means above all to come to terms with others, and to reconcile their needs with ours. That will in turn require a fine appreciation of what they regard as material to their unhindered existence. The present political weakness of the Soviet Union, its economic exhaustion, and its conversion to responsible behaviour within the international community have given us the opportunity. We hope that the opportunity will outlast those weaknesses, but it most certainly will not if we seek to exploit or prolong them.

On the contrary, our own strategy should take into account the disadvantage experienced by the Soviet Union; it should aim both to reassure and to draw the Soviets more and more into the planning of a joint system which is seen to safeguard their security as much as ours. For that we need to base ourselves on a rigorous analysis of what the world and its perspectives look like as observed from Moscow. That kind of analysis is greatly different from the one traditionally applied to anticipate the moves of an adversary. It means entering deep into the psychology and character, the cultural context, the feelings and reactions of the subject, and oneself to experience his perceived reverses and humiliations.

The purpose of a xenocentric analysis is to decide on actions designed deliberately to lessen those frustrations, rather than—as in the past—to heighten them. We know that feelings of insecurity, of inferiority and imagined international hostility, encourage instability and ill-considered reactions. The laager-mentality of being alone in a hostile world has too often betrayed its victims in the past. Avoiding this syndrome is an essential part of the confidence-building process. Positive action to counter it is already part of common security. Xenocentric analysis then also becomes a tool that helps us to monitor the effects of the whole confidence building exercise.

That does not mean that we should lower our guard. It implies the same *pari passu* approach as we have adpoted in the INF, CFE and START negotiations. Each step must be aimed at a specific result, and the next one taken only when that has been achieved. Such a formula will also make what is basically a conciliatory stance more credible, and therefore more trustworthy. Its effectiveness has already been tested in those negotiations and in the achievement of successes with even the most complex issues, like verification measures or the declaration on chemical and bacteriological weapons.

The parallel between the two goes further. The essentially politico-psychological process of reducing estrangement, building confidence and clearing the way towards common security must be accompanied by mutual arms reductions to remove the military threat. We know, for instance, that the Soviets perceived the major physical threat to themselves as their encirclement by nuclear bases, both land and seaborne. NATO has already provided political assurances about its intentions. In parallel, the START agreement has begun the process of deep mutual cuts in such weapons. At the same time the CFE treaty has reduced Soviet superiority in conventional weapons, which are the substance of the land-based attack for so long perceived by the West as the major threat.

The defence reviews undertaken by all NATO countries—except

possibly France—are intended to answer the question: what is the most cost-effective means of honouring our obligations and helping to counter a decreasing threat? Some, like the UK and France, have at the same time a concern for out-of-area problems which may pose threats of a different and unpredictable order. The answers have varied, often justifying percentage cuts in expenditure rather than making new dispositions, let alone touching sacred cows. Most, however, have made the assumption that negotiated reductions will in any event lighten the burden and make some restructuring necessary.

By that route they have come closer to certain concepts which have gained currency over recent times. 'Alternative defence' had envisaged precisely the type of scaled down and mobile permanent forces, capable of being quickly reinforced with reservists, which most countries now advocate. New technologies, particularly in missiles, have made it possible to develop cost-effective, and equally mobile, defensive systems against conventional attacks. Such forces and weapons also have the advantage that they can be rapidly deployed overseas. They therefore appear, fortuitously, to offer the best response to our foreseeable needs.

Seen from the Soviet side, such a development must seem reassuring. So long as the removal of tactical nuclear weapons is concluded, and the reduction of intermediate and strategic ones proceeds, anything aimed at repulsing a conventional attack does not constitute a threat. They are patently defensive and, unless the USSR does have the intent to launch a conventional offensive, they cannot be considered a challenge. It is, as the term implies, 'Non-provocative defence'.

But other measures are still wanted to make it effective. Open dialogue, necessary to remove imaginary threats, needs to be accompanied by open books to dispel real ones. Elsewhere we have noted that, in a non-confrontational order, there is security in ensuring that friend and adversary understand how our system works, and how it is activated. Since the new system does not rely on major fixed installations, inspections could be offered without sacrificing security or exposure to possible attack. Information—also, of course, on a reciprocal basis—could be provided about force levels and weapon capabilities. Procedures agreed within the CFE negotiations are likely to require such exchanges in any event.

None of this is intended to ignore the complexities involved in detailed planning of an adequate defence capability, especially for the UK and the USA where large naval establishments further complicate the issue. Or for the UK and France in the problems of maintaining, and possibly modernising, their independent deterrents. All these considerations are publicly available, even to the Soviets, for they are regularly discussed, scrutinised and published. We are here concerned only with suggesting the general directions in which it is appropriate to respond to the new situation in Europe, and to the task of building our future common security.

A final requirement is that of not remaining Euro-centric. If we are building the future, we must take into account also what threats it may hold from elsewhere. A new strategy must therefore consider out-of-area contingencies, even though the system we devise may not itself be part of the solution.

New strategy goals

In previous chapters we have already identified not only the main considerations but also the policy goals which might usefully now be adopted. They can be conveniently summarised here and grouped under appropriate headings for action.

The most urgent **political goals** would be those relating to the Soviet Union. They might be crystallised into the following:

– To signal an end to the system of opposing blocs, and to devise a set of actions to emphasise this intent.
– To give the Soviet leaders a feeling of belonging to Europe and avoid their isolation. Some have asked privately that the USSR should be given 'docking points', i.e. points where it can lock itself into collaboration with the West.
– To give Soviet leaders some successes to take home. So far, most actions and agreements, from Afghanistan to CFE and Stavropol, have on balance brought greater advantages for the West.
– To help the Soviets design a looser form of union which can serve to keep them together and avoid the dangers of the collapse of their state. The experience of the EC could be a material signpost.
– To devise a system which will give the dissident outer republics a political framework to which to belong, even if they remain within a more flexible Soviet state structure.

A further set of political goals relates to the pan-European field:

– We need to ensure that we work with, instead of opposing, the movement towards larger political units. The pooling of sovereignties will be as vital in eastern Europe as it has proved within the EC.

- New initiatives aimed at creating and maintaining order, and those involving eastern Europe in particular, need to be based on introducing the principles of democracy into relations between states.
- New systems should have a particular concern with the resolution of minority problems. They should permit minorities to feel more secure and allow them space to develop their interests and contacts with similarly placed peoples in the West.
- All countries concerned with Europe, including the US and USSR, should belong to a new security structure. This should in particular provide a productive framework for the new Germany, thus implicitly offering both the US and USSR reassurances about their respective security concerns.

Within the alliance itself, it is important:

- To maintain a consensus on eastern Europe, west European integration, and a partnership for global stability.
- To ensure that a significant US presence remains in Europe. To achieve this, the cost to the US will need to be drastically reduced.
- To build the European pillar of NATO. For the time being, it can be based on a WEU whose structure is suitably blended with NATO's. The EC would provide the political guidance, which will also be reconcilable with the neutrals among its present and future membership.

The principal **economic goals** would be:

- To assist eastern Europe to adjust its economies and practices so as to become first IMF-compatible, then EC-compatible.
- To extend cost-effective help to the Soviet economy, principally with management assistance to make its more important sectors work properly. Remember that the New Economic Policy of 1921 already once before sought to replace belligerent communism by restoring some commercial freedom and reverting to a market economy. We should avoid the clock being turned back a second time for lack of results.
- To support the developing Europe of the regions by encouraging economic operators, business and voluntary organisations, local

authorities and others to become involved at this level. This will help to link them into the new European space.

- To counter the dislocations arising from arms reductions. Research needs to be promoted into the fields of technology which offer readily available alternatives for investment, employment and profits.

The **strategic goals** which emerge are equally few and simple:

- Nuclear war is no longer an option, though it remains a possibility. Meanwhile the need is less for armies and more for co-operative policing.
- Forces can therefore be smaller, mobile and more versatile. That allows the introduction of 'alternative defence' as the strategic concept.
- Role specialisation can be conveniently linked with that concept. It will make not only for greater cost-effectiveness but should reduce potential tensions within NATO, especially by posing the need for a more closely integrated command structure.
- That structure will be a compelling operational reason for building a strong European pillar within NATO.

There are also a number of **out-of-area goals**. These apply less to NATO, which is unlikely to have a role outside Europe, but are of material concern to the alliance:

- To staunch the flow of arms to the Third World. This too may involve a search for alternative production and business opportunities offering comparable profits.
- To take urgent and determined action to prevent nuclear proliferation. Methods must also be found to deal with the threat from Third World countries already close to having their own nuclear capability.

Out-of-area concerns will be looked at separately later in this chapter. They are mentioned here principally because the action required involves the Soviet Union; it can therefore become part of the strategy implementation process examined below.

New strategy implementation

Implementation of a new strategy is equivalent to progressing towards a common security policy. There are five distinct and sequential steps in building such a policy and putting it into operation:

- Threat removal through sustained arms reductions;
- Confidence-building through joint problem solving;
- Collaborative planning mechanisms;
- Joint peace-keeping exercises;
- An institutional framework for collective security.

In the **arms reduction process** it will be important to strike a balance between national defence reductions and those still to be negotiated, otherwise there will not be enough leeway to strike bargains. The NATO FPP mechanism is the best adapted to ensuring that this does not happen and that a collective approach is maintained. This would achieve the desirable objective of co-ordination between the FPP and arms control, which even the reinforced High-Level Task Force has not yet fully realised.

It should be remembered that the first CFE treaty has been largely NATO's gain. Numerically, the Warsaw Pact is to remove ten times more treaty-listed items than NATO's expected 8000. The resulting effects on Soviet deployment will give NATO substantial benefits in predictability and warning time. Some concessions might have to be made in the next round, but care should be taken to ensure that there is no permanent link between numbers of US troops in Europe and Soviet troops stationed outside the USSR.

New fields are waiting to be opened up in **confidence-building**. In the first instance this should build on the measures already agreed in Stockholm, which have been working well in practice since 1986. To information about major manoeuvres might soon be added joint field exercises. Inspections, visits and exchanges are already provided for in the INF agreements. All these will serve to open up security arrangements and allow valuable insights.

The next stage should be a more proactive approach. It could begin with joint exercises in crisis management, of the kind which are held within NATO. They can initiate the practice of joint problem solving and give the military and diplomatic personnel involved invaluable lessons in the thinking, reactions and practices developed by others. It is important to recognise that both sides have much to learn from this. This would be a prelude to the proposal for greater collaboration between defence industries, and the provision of western management and technical assistance to Soviet industry, including the less sensitive areas concerned with defence.

Promotion of a mutual understanding of the processes concerned with defence would be deepened through **collaborative planning**

mechanisms. These could be structured to involve several stages. The first might be the exchange of strategic and technical doctrines. This would illustrate how each system functions and what is required to activate it. By doing that, a basis would be laid for actual joint planning. A complementary step would then be to institute procedures for regular working sessions between officials from NATO and the Warsaw Pact. These could progressively move to higher levels.

The most productive action would come in applying the insights gained of each other's strategic concepts to the development of a common European security doctrine. And that, in turn, could lead to jointly planning the application of the 'defensive sufficiency' concept and the dispositions for 'alternative defence'. At the outset that would entail a joint exercise to plan the dispositions on both sides, as if concerned with joint manoeuvres. In time, logic would alter the scope to the planning of joint dispositions to deal with more probable localised threats.

The concept would also follow the step-by-step principle, and therefore be progressive and controllable. Its justification rests on the fact that neither side will gain an advantage over the other. But both will become conditioned by useful experiences capable of being applied to crisis control and future peace-keeping.

The process can therefore be a valuable prelude to **joint peace-keeping exercises**. Some blueprints, such as the Eyskens plan, already exist for a European peace-keeping force. The Iraq crisis has offered an undesired but nonetheless valuable live test for such an action. In future, the proposed multinational corps would also provide appropriate experience for units to be attached to this type of mission, whether as UN blue berets or under any other auspices.

Finally, the **institutional framework for collective security** needs also to respect certain criteria. First, and by far the most important, is that all European countries and those intimately concerned with Europe must be members. That includes the USA and also the Soviet Union, both as full and active members. The latter is particularly important to prevent it feeling isolated and cut off from the West. Membership should also be open to all other European countries which may gain sovereignty or independence.

The CSCE has attracted the greatest consensus as the framework best adapted to this task. As the harbinger of respect for human rights in eastern Europe it already possesses the necessary prestige. It also enjoys the full membership of all those currently capable of belonging to it.

CSCE now needs to be invested with appropriate responsibilities, and the organs making it capable of discharging them. Whilst we should beware of creating new institutions, we should also be liberal in ensuring that CSCE is endowed with all the agencies it needs to become sufficiently prestigious to command compliance by its members. Its Conflict Prevention Centre will begin by adding conciliation and risk reduction to the process of confidence building. In due course, however, it should become capable of answering complaints and, in the last resort, authorising the intervention of peace-keeping forces.

To assist CSCE to bear those increasingly grave responsibilities, it will be useful progressively to transfer some appropriate functions to it. The more immediate ones would be the inspections and verification procedures under the CFE agreements.

A cardinal requirement is that any such institution should be able to achieve permanence. It can do this only by lending itself to continual adaptation as circumstances arise which we cannot as yet predict. It would be a tragedy if our new institution failed to perform in a few years' time because we had prematurely encased it in concrete. Here too the EC model, with its progressive growing together, can be relevant. It could have the added advantage that CSCE might in time become its mirror image.

The world out-of-area

It is evident that the Third World—in general the developing countries of the southern hemisphere—is bristling with causes for conflict. At any given moment, a number of long-festering military engagements are being bitterly fought out. A count of close on 200 wars fought since the end of the Second World War places at least 90 per cent within that area. Between them they have cost 22 million lives, mostly of civilians. All that has been said in previous chapters about the instabilities created by minorities, the strife over frontiers excited by newly independent states, exploited by superpower rivalries, applies with double force to the developing world.

The process has been richly fuelled and abetted by poverty, arms sales and the relatively recent phenomenon of indebtedness. The launching of scores of new countries during the post-war wave of independence, armed with little more than the western concept of nationalism—so ill-fitting with their real demography—has institutionalised poverty. Most of them lack the resources for real independence. However onerous the regime of colonialism, severing those links just at the point where they were needed for economic take-off was a victory of optimism over reason.

Poverty has, in fact, compounded the dependence. Links with the metropolitan country which, however ignominious, brought markets and investment have been replaced by the perennial need for aid. Aid and the dependence on it bring more shame and resentment. Many governments, unable to master their economic problems, have openly used that resentment to gloss over their failures and maintain power over peoples becoming ever poorer. They have lost control over population growth, recognised too late as a peril rather than a symbol of national virility. Many of the smaller countries have become marginalised and irrelevant to the world outside.

The witches' gift of nationalism laid in their cradle has led to strife, rather than co-operation, with neighbours. That has created an appetite for weaponry and mini-arms races between them. Suppliers of arms and merchandise, as well as lenders for ambitious development projects, have kept careful accounts. Those debts were compounded when, as a result of successive oil crises, banks had to offload huge balances and urgently find borrowers. For some countries the total debt burden has become intolerable. Merely to keep up with interest payments diverts huge resources from their own development. The creditor bravely maintains the fiction that at least part of the principal is secure; but it would need only one major real default to explode that also.

Meanwhile we have seen the first war ignited by debt. Iraq's huge borrowings, principally to pay for its campaign against Iran, could not be serviced from oil sales whilst allowing it to satisfy its other ambitions. What lay easier to hand than to seize one of its largest creditors by the throat and take all his assets for good measure? Even for countries with vast resources like Iraq, the failure to create economic well-being at home encourages international adventures. Moreover, nationalism blinds its victims, and instability effectively blocks constructive dialogue. Such situations can lead only to the disaster necessary to produce a final purge.

The lesson of interdependence, bought so dearly and with so much blood by Europeans, has still to be absorbed in the Third World. Here and there, the signs are positive. There is a new realism in relations with the North, in part a reflection of the lessening rivalry between the superpowers. There is a mirroring of the eastern European abandonment of communism and one-party rule, and a consequent disenchantment with Europe's second malicious baptismal gift, the brand of socialism that justified repression. In some areas at least, there is a return to regional co-operation with neighbours confronting the same problems. There is a new realism within the UN, spearheaded by the restored purposefulness of the Security Council.

But, as in eastern Europe, adjustment to the after-shocks of the fall of communism is provoking new instabilities. Throughout much of Africa, the old autocracies are trembling. Reform and realignments are still to come in the two Koreas. The catharsis of China cannot be long delayed. Vietnam and Cambodia remain to be stabilised. The spread of 'communist' insurgency in the Philippines has yet to be reversed.

Are the real dramas of the world now likely to unfold in the Third World, propelled by the new enemies of poverty, population and, in consequence, pollution and the threat to the global environment? The statistics of environmental degradation, of the slaughter of forests, the progress of desertification, the shifting climate demonstrate the threat to the world as a whole. Rural populations are getting poorer, with rapidly decreasing resources of land and fuel having to serve ever-increasing numbers. As once they were born into slavery, millions are now born into the bondage of poverty.

Terms such as 'out-of-area' have a bizarre ring of irrelevance before such tragedies. Yet the connection is immediate. If problems have become global, posing threats to our security and long-term existence, can we really distinguish between in-area and out-of-area? We are immediately involved at four levels: economic, political, environmental, and security.

At the economic level, we have to combat poverty, transfer substantial resources, and provide economic assistance, no longer just with the heart, but for the most hard-headed of reasons. That means rethinking what we term 'aid', much of which, however humanitarian, may well be counter-productive by dulling the instinct for self-help. Assistance in creating economic wealth, and with it the resources for self-help, has long been an objective. But it has not been backed up with insistence on the adoption of sufficiently rigorous economic and individual disciplines which make this western process work in the West.

Largely due to the many conflicting voices and lobbies, western aid policies are a mess. They rest on the pretence that, since one is dealing with sovereign states, any political interference is not permissible. Yet the whole of the development process which we sustain is played out in the political, and not the economic arena. We connive at a process of political change, but are too coy to acknowledge it. Rather than to risk doing that, we prefer to stand aloof and condemn our resource transfers to the obscure sinks into which they drain.

Relations with the many developing countries to which this applies—but by no means all—need to be placed on a politically more adult relationship. They should contain a greatly increased measure of guidance and a greater definition of, and adherence to, common objectives. To be sure, the West—as its own fluctuating performance has shown—is not infallible, nor incorruptible. But western techniques have grown out of a different environment and ethic, and the growing medium as well as the plant needs to be transferred.

Such political understandings become more urgently necessary as we begin to confront the common task of husbanding the environment. Here too one encounters natural sensitivities. Yet the British understanding with Brazil on the issue of Amazonian rainforests has shown how these can be intelligently overcome. All these matters require trade-offs and some reciprocity. One cannot promote more efficient production and then deny it markets. One cannot preach conservation of forests and then demand that one's debts be serviced in hard currency which only that timber can buy. And finally, one cannot persuade countries to switch expenditure from arms, to development and leave them at the mercy of the local bully.

Tasks for the Alliance

What does all this portend for the Atlantic alliance, or indeed for a future pan-European security system? We must consider two separate sets of problems which may arise: those involving the NATO flanks, and those totally out-of-area but posing threats for individual members of the alliance.

The Iraqi threat on Turkey's borders has already illustrated the complexities which arise over such issues. The threat to a NATO member elicits a clear and unequivocal answer. But the aggressor has other dimensions and has to be dealt with on other fronts. Even if his principal or only target had been Turkey, a NATO action would have assumed an out-of-area character. The same blockade, the same alliances with the enemy's Arab neighbours would have had to be invoked, the same protective action launched. Where then does 'out-of-area' begin?

A similar, though graver, problem might arise in the case of an attack upon Israel. The USA, as well as several European countries, might feel called upon to intervene. But so—at some future hypothetical date when its Muslim population had assumed decisive and possibly belligerent proportions—might the USSR, perhaps on the other side. Problems could equally arise in the Maghreb, which might be perceived as threats by France, Spain and Italy—but by few of their other partners.

All these could create tensions and possible disunity among NATO members. On many such issues it could be difficult to arrive at a European-Atlantic consensus, far less at agreed action. Even more severe differences would manifest themselves if the Soviet Union were at some stage to oppose the western line.

Such tensions must clearly be pre-empted well before they can arise. The kind of crisis management exercises proposed above, to be held jointly with the Soviet Union, would offer a practical instrument. If they were to concentrate also on fringe and out-of-area problems, they should help to overcome the element of surprise and lead to the development of known, if not always common, responses. The Soviet Union's decision to cease profiting from worldwide instability at the expense of the West has made it possible to envisage an eventual co-management of the world's security problems.

The changed attitude has been manifest over Iraq and in the Bush–Gorbachev call for peace initiatives in the Horn of Africa and Angola. It is a promising signpost that the USSR might be ready to embark on such joint exercises. But skill will be needed to ensure that this does not send the wrong signals to the Third World, images of the prosperous North ganging up against the impoverished South. Nor must it be seen as a common front against newly perceived threats, such as Muslim fundamentalism, highlighted only to keep the superpowers' military machines in action.

Some of these suspicions could be allayed if the declared object were to ensure swifter decision making within the UN Security Council. The exercises would then also provide some answers for a potential contribution of NATO members to future UN peace-keeping forces. The UN has already become rather better at organising these and its role has gained a new prestige. This could be greatly consolidated by promoting preliminary understandings between East and West on responses to emergencies in specific areas.

Action on nuclear proliferation

In addition to the five acknowledged nuclear powers, there are now estimated to be at least 14 already possessing a more or less fully developed nuclear weapons system—like Israel, Libya, Pakistan and South Africa—or able to develop one within a measurable time if they chose. Such capabilities would not have been developed without a purpose. At the very least, that would be to intimidate potential aggressors. Yet where that perceived attacker has himself obtained a nuclear capacity—as between India and Pakistan, or Israel, Libya and perhaps tomorrow Iraq—the danger level is acute. Having all but banished the spectre of nuclear war in Europe, we may yet witness it becoming a reality in Third World conflicts.

Worse, we may find that future locally ignited wars can escalate into that long-dreaded global nuclear holocaust. A Third World nuclear adventurer may force his opponent into submission, then use the same nuclear blackmail against others coming to his aid. European territory could already be vulnerable to such weapons, and will increasingly become so as delivery systems are improved.

Is there still time to forestall this, and to make a renewed attempt for wider adherence to the Nuclear Non-Proliferation Treaty? A special conference of signatory members is intended to meet in 1995 to discuss the future of the treaty. Time is ticking away with greater urgency than this. One hopeful sign is that France at least sent an observer to the penultimate review meeting in 1990, although this ended without an agreed document. Its independent policy is based on trade-offs between non-proliferation of weapons and the development of civil applications of atomic energy, in other words, commercial opportunities. Yet those peaceful uses have led directly to the rise of the new generation of Third World nuclear powers.

It is fairly clear that a new initiative is needed to bring countries like China, India, Pakistan, Brazil, Argentina and Korea—to name but a few—to sign the treaty. NATO cannot do this on its own but, because of its technical competence and structure, it should be able to co-ordinate western political action in this field.

Equally urgent is the task of curbing the sale of technology and fissile material. The main offenders are western Europe, the Soviet Union, China and Japan. The Chinese in particular are selling missiles and materials to anyone who wants them; they have become an invaluable source of revenue for the party organisation. Although action here lies in the commercial field, the stakes are high and governments under pressure. Yet the USA has already shown that it is possible to resist these temptations.

Another requirement should be that the existing signatories respect their obligations. They undertook to effect negotiated reductions in their forces. Yet the UK, and France also, are actually planning through modernisation to increase the destructive power of their nuclear forces. That may just be in accordance with the letter, hardly with the spirit of an agreement through which it is hoped that others will actually renounce what they already possess. A formula to convince those others could be to call a comprehensive test ban, but that would itself mean some very hard bargaining, particularly with the USA, UK and France.

Action to enforce commercial disciplines on producer countries is best taken within the International Atomic Energy Agency (IAEA) in Vienna. It would be a hopeful sign if this could be prompted by a decision of Euratom, committing the EC as a whole. IAEA would then be in a powerful position to intercede with the non-members, China and Japan. The NATO alliance, if not through NATO itself, has a powerful role to play. Talks about the proliferation problem are already in train between the US and USSR. It is imperative that other NATO members should co-operate in this endeavour.

The role of Japan

Japan is undergoing a psychological crisis. Its post-war constitution renounced collective security, nuclear weapons, and military engagement beyond its own borders. These prohibitions have excluded it from many of the world's councils and produced a sense of isolation. That has only been heightened by its technological and commercial success. No doubt the freedom from having to shoulder defence burdens contributed to that success, but it is now conscious of being the country 'without a foreign policy'.

Yet it has some very legitimate security interests alongside the European ones. There is a continual danger that East–West arms reduction agreements will merely shift the Soviet arsenal east of the Urals, thence to threaten the Pacific. The Soviet Union has made conciliatory moves in the area, notably towards Korea and China, with agreed reductions of forces on their border. Yet Japanese observers appear less than optimistic about a real softening of Soviet policy.

Japan's dilemma was newly emphasised during the Iraq crisis.

Deputy foreign minister Takakazu Kuriyama was moved to comment, 'With Japan's international position and responsibilities, it would not be correct to honour our obligations solely with financial help.' A general of the self-defence force put it more emotionally, 'We cannot pretend to be part of the free world, if we are not ready to shed our blood to protect world security. Japan cannot be content merely to furnish a financial contribution.'

It is doubtful whether Japan's Asian neighbours would agree. Although attempts to send even non-combatant units to the Gulf have already had a rough passage within Japan itself, any change in her defence posture would still be viewed with some alarm. On the other hand, what would happen if Korea were to put the finishing touches to its nuclear capability? What would be the reaction of Japan, whose technology in nuclear power, reprocessing and launcher systems would very swiftly allow it to perfect a nuclear weapon? With a rogue force in its midst, how would the Asian community then view Japanese rearmament? And what would be the effect on NATO members, or on the USSR?

Concurrently, there is mounting hostility to the US presence in Korea, the Philippines and Japan. This is adding to US worries that Japan's economic preponderance in south-east Asia could become destabilising. It aggravates a situation made already highly sensitive by Japanese commercial intrusion into the USA itself.

Happily, Japan has itself requested some form of consultative status with NATO, to be associated with any development of NATO's political dimension, and involved in negotiations on arms reductions. It has tried to stake a claim even in formulating western policies towards eastern Europe and the USSR. Such participation could, of course, make these processes more cumbersome. On the other hand, it will be a wholesome reminder that there is another world out there which also has a view.

The most positive aspect, however, is that working together on common problems will make it possible to enlist Japan more readily in other actions. Curbing the sale of nuclear technology and fissile material is one such. Using its good offices to persuade other Asian nations to join the non-proliferation treaty is a second. And a not negligible third is in having a forum in which to discuss any eventual nuclear plans by Japan herself.

Stemming the arms trade

Trade in conventional arms has reached alarming proportions, as has the steep growth in the number of supplier countries. At one time mainly in the hands of the US, USSR and UK, it expanded swiftly in the years of the oil crises when both eastern and western Europe seriously entered the field. Since then they have been joined by relatively new, but by now highly significant Third World suppliers like Brazil and South Africa. The trade has been helped by sophisticated financing arrangements, from counter-trade to offset deals.

Prospects for stemming the supply either at source or at secondary black market level are gloomy. East–West arms reductions will provide a further impetus to an already flourishing trade. In any event, a large proportion of transfers to the Third World is represented by official military aid. Few if any of these sources will be happy to co-operate in an impervious limitation agreement.

The improvement in the stance of the Soviet Union in relation to Third World conflicts has nevertheless opened up new possibilities. Mr Gorbachev has been a keen supporter of UN peace-keeping efforts and has even aimed to resuscitate the UN Military Staff Committee to act as a high command for Security Council peace-keeping operations. This, and the evident willingness of the Soviet Union to reach understandings with the US, can provide a basis for enlisting the authority of the UN in attempts at conventional arms control.

In an important contribution to this subject, Edward J Streator[12] has put forward the concept of regional bodies, supported by the UN, to promote restraint among recipients themselves. Such bodies would need a growing consensus among the US and USSR about their purposes, and support through voluntary limitation of superpower arms supplies into their area. The major regional powers should be encouraged to provide a lead, especially in sponsoring regional agreements for arms transfer limitations, and eventually giving those bodies a peace-making role and regional verification regimes.

It is clear that such an initiative could not succeed without the support of NATO members. Once more, NATO with the USSR and other Warsaw Pact members who are substantial arms suppliers, should ensure agreement and then support it within the UN. The problem will not, of course, go away. It will still be there for the new pan-European security body to monitor in the future.

The predominance of the commercial interests involved again raises the question of how peace can be made more profitable. For the developing countries the answer may lie in a system of rewards and penalties. Bodies like the IMF and World Bank are in a position to monitor—though not stop—a good part of this trade, and the subsequent use of the arms. If there were regional bodies with some authority in the matter, they would establish a legal framework for aid to be trimmed in accordance with compliance.

There is also the potential peace dividend, calculated at US$50 billion on the basis of a 5 per cent worldwide cut. It is, of course, idle to pretend that more than an infinitesimal fraction would find its way to the Third World. So far, we have remunerated those who bought our arms. Would it be possible (and cheaper in the end) to pay them not to? More especially if they were able to show that they had made matching savings? In any event, a good deal of decommissioned equipment could be transferred as a basis for regional disaster relief pools, possibly under UN auspices to ensure adequate maintenance.

For the industrial countries the incentives are more difficult to devise. Here no one will legislate or willingly devise incentives. The new system will have to arise out of the inevitable dislocations in the defence industries themselves. They will release considerable scientific and technical resources. Some way should be found to assist their redeployment in allied growth areas such as electronics, information technology and telecommunications.

We would, however, be failing if we did not ensure that the next generation is trained to take advantage of the areas now being opened up by research in other fields of endeavour. Advances in genetic engineering, backed up by new botanical achievements, are ready to be taken out of the laboratory to deliver another green revolution. They can also cut the need for fertilisers, and hence reduce pollution. New therapies from natural proteins, engineering proteins to make food, production of new molecules, all are the heralds of those sciences and their products with which we need to replace the smokestack industries of the Cold War age.

There too is a peaceable relationship with the Third World. We are on the edge of a botanical revolution where, for instance, feed grain can now be grown even on salt marshes. For populous developing countries that can overcome the limitations of rice and provide an addition of animal proteins to the diet. Perhaps man's ingenuity may yet find a way to feed those extra mouths—before they succumb to starvation, or perish in the wars visited upon them by their discontented masters.

The implications for the new strategy

It would be easy to look at the turbulence of the southern hemisphere and decide that we could not, after all, reduce our arms or preparedness. The potential threats are legion and on a scale from brush-fire wars to full-scale nuclear aggression.

Yet there are substantial similarities between the situation in Europe and that in the Third World. In Europe, the threat and confrontation happen to be in retreat; in the Third World, they are in the ascendant. Yet, as always, the causes lie in human nature and in the way it drives relations between states. The factors we have diagnosed bear a considerable resemblance to each other, wherever they appear. So we need to look at our situation more calmly.

The first imperative is to distinguish between risks and threats. On closer examination, relatively few potential trouble-spots will reveal themselves as recognisable threats demanding our intervention.

Secondly, we have to analyse the threats and decide which could in fact be dealt with by military means. We shall no doubt find that events in Cambodia or Burma (Myanmar), in Haiti or Peru, in Angola or Djibouti, would not yield to military force. In most cases we shall have to acknowledge that the only contribution we can make is a political, or politico-economic one.

When we have thus cleared our minds, we shall also have isolated the real danger spots and may then be better able to judge the kind of weaponry we shall need. That may look remarkably like our new forces in Europe, with the addition of long-haul naval and airborne transport capacity.

Our analysis is also likely to support the need for a strengthening of the UN's peace-keeping capacity, based on East–West understandings and the progressive practice of joint crisis management exercises. These will reveal more clearly the urgency for joint action to prevent and abate nuclear proliferation, whilst throttling back the trade in conventional arms.

With that, we shall have a strategy which is at least complete and coherent. It will not be unassailable. But its strength will lie in making allies of former enemies, whilst creating a world system to deter those with the ambition to become new ones.

10

Coming Back to NATO

'Everything is in flux; change is the only reality.'

HERACLITUS OF EPHESUS

In a perfect world . . .

One of the characteristics of our times is the continual search for improvement in our institutional structures. Our critical faculties have become highly developed and are ready to seize upon the patent weaknesses we see. We can debate at length the failings of the many and mighty edifices we have built since the end of the Second World War to make ours a better world. From the UN downwards, we lament their lethargy, or their impotence to deal with this or that situation.

Familiarity with the order imposed upon the one-time chaos of international affairs has cost us the perspective of seeing what the world could still be like without them. We can freely criticise the policeman, bemoan the rising tide of crime, agitate for more to be done to ensure our immunity from molestation. We no longer remember those Dickensian times when our own world, let alone the far-flung rest of it, was peopled with brigands, footpads and freebooters. Nor are Anglo-Saxons conscious of how recent, and how rare, is the prize of being able to criticise at all.

Thus the trees of imperfection obscure our view of the wood of protection, in whose shade we can live out our more or less tranquil lives. The concept of war, of general mobilisation robbing every family in the land of its able-bodied men—temporarily and too often permanently—has all but vanished from our field of possibilities. Crises are a media product. In any event, those that are real are for others to resolve.

In short, we have arrogated to ourselves the right to demand perfection, mostly without counting the cost in terms of the forfeits to be traded, of other freedoms foregone, and of sovereignties diminished. We know exactly what 'they' should do, but are less than clear about what is demanded from us in return. Let us then consider how things might look in an ideal world—a world in which the major obstacles of the past have yielded, and all players would refrain from creating new ones to impede progress towards an improved set of rules and a better game.

First, we would devise a system of security which is not based on the insecurity of others. We would respect the wishes of eastern Europe and the needs of the Soviet Union. We would no longer expect the Soviets to negotiate on nuclear matters as if the US were their only enemy. We would have to bring in others. China's nuclear force is hard up against the USSR's eastern frontier. The UK and France seem intent on increasing the power of theirs. The USSR may not like to live with a fiction of the kind which makes the Bonn–Paris axis the backbone of Europe, has set up the Franco-German defence council and given birth to the Franco-German brigade—yet keeps French Pluton missiles targeted on West German territory.

Secondly, we would act swiftly to ensure that the US stays in Europe. It will not be enough that they should do this because they feel their own security is at stake. Perceptions of that may change with time, and with events in their own hemisphere or the Pacific rim. We want them to feel fully involved in the future of Europe. We want them to believe that they are a European power. It was Churchill and Roosevelt's achievement to bring the US back into a Europe from which it had severed itself. Thanks to the Cold War, their successors were able to extend its presence over half a century.

That identity may be more difficult to maintain in the future. We can probably cope with the economic disincentives of the budget deficit and the political ones of feeling that it is time for Europe to grow up and work more coherently for its own defence. Those are the strictures of an east coast establishment weary with the gaggle of old world relatives still seeking to send their bills to the nephew who made his fortune in the new. Less easy to counter will be the demographic shift, with opinion residing more and more firmly in Texas and an hispanophone California. Soon more than half of all Americans will speak Spanish; they may well have a very different agenda. That will become reflected in Washington, where the burgeoning populations of such states as these will, for the first time, give the West a greater representation than the East.

In our ideal world, we would overcome that by offering the US parity in the task of protecting our common interests in Europe. We would rapidly build the European pillar of NATO for the common security. And we would proffer a similar pillar to the alliance, by decking out our European Community with economic and political union. By that process, we shall make it a pillar strong enough to carry the load, especially of the hard decisions that a common security policy—within NATO as well as beyond—would demand.

Thirdly, we would want the Soviet Union, too, to feel itself a European partner. Whatever its condition, we want to use its present open disposition to bind it firmly within the comity of responsible nations. No good saying, 'let's see if it lasts, or what comes out of it'. For 300 years, since Peter the Great, Russia has looked to secure openings to the West or, in Pushkin's words, 'to chop a window through to Europe'. That's why the Baltic states were so important— and still are, until a better relationship with the West can be devised. Today, the Soviet reformers use space language and ask to be given 'docking points'. What they mean by that, so descriptively, is opportunities to link into co-operation with us.

There too, the demographic factor is at work. Within a few years, more than half the population of the present Soviet Union will be Muslim. Moscow, Russia, the Ukraine have no wish to become Asian. Their traditions lie elsewhere. They want western influences to overcome the national resistance to change, not the Asian ones. If we fail to respond, Pushkin's realistic phrase may again become the solution. We should not forget that the defection of all of eastern Europe has deprived the USSR of its western contacts and observation posts.

Peter the Great imported German craftsmen, Dutch shipbuilders and French manners to modernise his empire. Mr Gorbachev, and Mr Yeltsin even more, have begun to open the doors to western capital and expertise. Both have aimed, at different speeds, to launch a revolution as profound as that which most of eastern Europe underwent in 1989. It is a western revolution, without ideology and led by pragmatism. We have an option to speed it on its way, work with it, help it to register the successes it needs to rally new recruits. In our ideal world, we would have the wisdom to take it. Not out of emotion or idealism, but on the same terms as they are offering: as good business to build a world safe for capitalism and to share in its spoils.

Lastly, we would look to the logic of all these criteria in asking ourselves what role we see for Europe itself, that hesitant colossus lying between the two colossi to east and west. And that, finally, will show us what we need to ask of NATO in the times that lie ahead.

A pattern of Europe

A first glance at current relationships reveals a somewhat confused litter of organisations, institutions and other bodies with varying or overlapping memberships, competences and authorities. All are attempts to achieve a degree of joint endeavour; most are expressions of the search for greater unity of purpose, a very few of the will to reach a larger, more structured unity. It is not necessary to dwell on the reasons for the proliferation, nor for the arrested growth of some, or the halting progress of others.

When we study these organisms more closely, we begin to see the elements of an emerging pattern. We find not only a common inspiration, but relationships which, here and there, are proactive and complementary, rather than competitive or countervailing. With a little more optimism, we see that they are capable, indeed, of being arranged more or less functionally. We begin to see some possible substance in the concept of concentric circles. All that is missing, perhaps, is the capacity to see the pattern four-dimensionally, with a time element introduced to make it more intelligible.

With this in mind, let us look at a possible sequence of events, in the hope of fashioning the circles to make a chain that can effectively bind us to a common future.

The first priority, then, is to use the **CFE talks** to negotiate further reductions of force levels and eliminate offensive capacities, but to do so multilaterally. That will continue to need a deal of co-ordination within NATO. So will the transition from bloc-to-bloc negotiations to participation of their individual members, to ensure the orderly withdrawal of all Soviet troops to their own territory.

At some stage during this process we shall also come to the blending of **CFE into CSCE**. This will begin with verification and the use of multinational inspection teams. These functions could be progressively transferred to CSCE, within which such teams could develop further into eventual peace-keeping forces. A second occasion would present itself within the CFE to assist the Soviet buffer states (Poland, Hungary, Czechoslovakia, Bulgaria, Romania), not only through the departure of Soviet troops but by enabling them to make do with a minimal level of forces. That would also provide the USSR with the additional security of knowing that they could not fight on anyone else's side. Their 'neutrality' needs, however, to be secured in some way, and the only one on offer is through the CSCE.

Meanwhile, we need to integrate European national defence efforts within **NATO**. This has to be achieved in such a way that each country makes a contribution appropriate to its ability. That is the doctrine of role specialisation, which makes it unnecessary for each country expensively to maintain all three services. In that way the cost of constructing NATO's European pillar could be kept within politically realistic bounds. The UK, for instance, would concentrate on a maritime and air force role; whilst the UK and French deterrents might eventually be merged into a single European one.

Integration of that kind will require a degree of intimacy and common purpose which only the **European Community** is likely to be able to summon. Some will rile at the loss of sovereignty or autonomy. Others will find it hard to come to terms with any cost-sharing formula or calculation of equivalent input. There will be pressures to protect the holy milch-cows of national defence industries. All that demands a large area of automatic and institutionalised agreement on economic and foreign policy, which is exactly what the EC now has high on its agenda. Equally, role specialisation would give a renewed impetus for rationalisation of the defence industry, the creation of a common market in defence equipment, and the work under way within the Independent European Programme Group. More single-assembly-line, multiple supplier projects like Airbus would further reduce the costs of an integrated defence effort.

It has been shown that the European pillar would, for the time being at least, rest upon the twin trestle of **EC** political control and **WEU** military co-ordination; and that in this the **European Parliament** and the **WEU Assembly** would assure an element of democratic scrutiny.

As NATO's European pillar, the EC and WEU would have to enter into a more far-reaching relationship with **NATO's flanks**, that is its European non-EC members. The EC is already associated with Norway through **EFTA**, whilst Turkey is an associate member, perhaps one day to become a full one. A similar role could be devised for Iceland, the more so as it has the affinity with France of not forming part of the integrated command structure. However, the link through WEU should be clear and positive.

There remains the all-important link between the **EC and the USA**. In part, this would clearly continue to lie within NATO. But there is also the aspect which has been expressed as 'the Alliance, and yet not NATO'. Until quite recently, relations between the two powers were conducted mainly in international trade bodies, or locked in gladiatorial combat over chickens or oilseeds. More recently, the EC's political dimension has become recognised, and never more clearly than during the Iraq crisis. The role of the EC as an important spokesman for Europe has been accepted.

The question now arises whether the alliance, or EC-USA relations, stand in need of being further cemented. As the EC assumes the format and functions of a superpower, frictions and inequities may arise which would be better for a settlement before they can become inflamed. Contingent problems span the whole spectrum of political, economic, trade and financial affairs. Banking regulations for 1992 and the single European market already threaten to assume that character.

One proposal is that they should enter into a treaty relationship. However, it seems that the habit of regarding the US as too powerful has not yet been broken. For the time being, the result has been limited to a joint declaration and more regular bilateral consultations. But our horizon is tomorrow and the day after that. Should we not be considering whether some of the institutions we have created for ourselves could in due course fructify the transatlantic relationship? What of machinery for settling disputes, a common economic watchdog when the EC assumes greater powers in this domain, and a financial and monetary one to harmonise actions by one which could damage the other? The **Group of Seven** might then automatically acquire a core group of two.

If European forces are integrated to the extent suggested, this would also imply common decision making in relation to the two theatres in which they may need to be deployed: peace-keeping within eastern Europe, especially to assure the security of the **CSCE's** eastern members; and **out-of-area** problems demanding a common western response. This in turn will require more politically efficient structures within **NATO**, within the **CSCE**, and under the auspices of the **UN and the Security Council**.

We can now see that our chain amounts to an efficient multi-tiered decision making structure, whose links are logically composed as follows:

- the EC-WEU European co-ordinating pillar within NATO;
- the EC politico-economic vector of the alliance, and its growing relationship of equality and co-operation with the USA;

- CSCE, which should progressively become supreme in reaching a consensus on European security matters and, in due course, capable of initiating action in support of it;
- a consultative mechanism, perhaps a NATO-USSR (or EC-USA-USSR) common security caucus, as a mechanism for involving the USSR in the practice of common decision making, crisis management and strategic planning;
- the use of this common security body to agree action to be taken on security matters within the CSCE area, as well as out-of-area where the context demands;
- joint action, also carefully prepared by such a body, within the UN Security Council.

Care would have to be exercised to avoid such a caucus being seen by the other CSCE members as anything but an effort to streamline its work and to provide it with a record of early successes. Whilst institutions and initiatives to further democratic principles, such as those already launched, will begin to establish the CSCE's authority, it must progressively be given teeth. These may start with voluntary conciliation, but need eventually to become mandatory, if CSCE is to become a real security organisation. Tacit co-operation by the major powers within it would send it off to a good start. The caucus might even, in time, become the CSCE's own security council.

Equally, in out-of-area matters it will be important not to give other Security Council members, far less the Third World as a whole, the impression that the whole power of the North is being arrayed against them. One way perhaps to avoid that is to enlist their co-operation in the kind of UN-sponsored regional bodies discussed in the previous chapter.

The portents for NATO

The world needs carefully to preserve what cohesion it has. The time for dissolving all pacts and alliances is therefore not yet. For the time being, NATO has a continuing mission to guarantee adequately the security of its members. Its resolve to do that by all means and against all comers must remain clearly visible. Above all, that requires the retention of a strong US involvement in Europe.

However, NATO must also back up the declaration of friendship extended to the Warsaw Pact and its leader with appropriate action. Some of this was already heralded by the London declaration. There must now be a broad move to enter into collaborative exercises, multilaterally with the Warsaw Pact—so long as it subsists—and bilaterally with the Soviet Union. NATO must play a positive role within a continuous CFE process, and take the initiative with well-balanced proposals for further arms reductions. It should be careful to ensure that these respect also the perceived needs of the USSR.

At the same time, NATO needs to plan for a progressive change in its role and objectives. Its future role will be to contribute to the preservation of stability in central and eastern Europe. It will do so by making a decisive technical contribution to the creation of a pan-European security system, possessing in particular some of the capacity needed to deal with local conflicts. It has to become an instrument for building trust, rather than exciting fear and suspicion.

Effectively, NATO has to embark on a gradual transition from shield-and-strike to becoming a European peace academy. Over time, its doctrine will emphasise peace-keeping rather than defence. It will have shared responsibility for creating the professional and institutional systems for that role, and for maintaining, and if necessary enforcing, the peace. The transition will be delicate, in particular the task of building confidence in its increasingly wider objectives and peaceable intent.

To a large extent, that will depend on the amount of political input and guidance *within* NATO. Neither ministers nor ambassadors have in the past gone much beyond their technical agendas. That will not do during the transition process, when strong political direction will be essential to safeguard the balance of actions in both fields. Lord Carrington, a former secretary general, has proposed to fill that gap with a political committee composed of ministers from the political level of their respective foreign offices. Their task would be to shape the future defence of the West and ensure that it corresponds to the unfolding pattern of events. That should clearly include the processes of adaptation and transition.

There will need to be other structural changes. It is clear that we have reached the limits of reliance on the US cavalry coming to Europe's aid when we have once again spilled our porridge. It is now our turn to relieve them. Europe's coming of age, and the EC's arrival at the age of consent, must be swiftly reflected in the construction of the European pillar within NATO. But that will demand further changes in NATO's structure and procedures. It must imply a greater streamlining towards swift one-on-one decisions, whilst not forgetting Canada and other non-EC members. That is what the pillar should be all about, however tough it proves at first to reach a consensus within it.

In summary, so long as the process of transition is neither clear nor complete, NATO will be needed as an expression of the West's political objectives in relation to its own defence and the building of new, and equally effective, collective security structures. It should be drafted into the confidence-building process and help to chart the way to a transition from a system of opposing blocs to one of common security. It is an instrument for negotiations on present, future and interim security arrangements. And it has a preponderant role in intra-alliance matters, most urgently in finding a new balance between the efforts of Europe and the USA.

'The Alliance, and yet not NATO'

From now on, most of the problems facing the NATO alliance, both internally and externally, are likely to be overwhelmingly political. The political alliance between the NATO members is irreplaceable, but the respective roles within it must change. In the same way as NATO faces the challenge of change, the alliance itself must move on.

Even internally, it is facing some daunting problems. There is the almost immediate one of the stationing of US troops and nuclear weapons. There is the question of modernisation of those weapons and the development of doctrines based on new ones like TASMs. Of course, these are classic NATO problems; but this time they have a more serious political dimension. They will be greatly dependent on the role and attitudes of the new Germany.

It is easy to be mesmerised by Germany's vital statistics. With virtually a quarter of the EC's population and gross domestic product, it is easy to develop fears about a possible independent or dominating role. Yet the danger lies less in our apprehensions than in the future perceptions of the German people of what their role should be. There is no indication of any historic military ambitions coming to the surface, and that possibility can safely be dismissed. On the contrary, the problems are likely to arise precisely because, with peace reigning and their objective of unification achieved, they want to see no more of war. That may include an end to foreign troops and bases on their soil.

The building of the European pillar, essential as it is, will inevitably not be achieved without further stresses. The integration of France within the pillar may have become more palatable through the ending of the system of opposing blocs, a greater acknowledgement of out-of-area risks, and the possible adoption of the *Force d'action rapide* as a model for the units required in Europe and elsewhere. But no one pretends that French political constraints on its defence philosophy will make it quick or easy.

Stresses will undoubtedly arise out of the very fact that the creation of the pillar will set the seal on the arrival, however reluctantly, of a new world power. Political, economic and then security integration will signal the EC's new status. The fact that, like its largest constituent, it is born of peace will only add to its full-grown stature. We would do well to ensure that action is taken to pre-empt some of the frictions that could arise from its insertion into the ranks of world powers. Not only relations with the US, as we have seen, should be endowed with instruments for arbitration, but also those with Japan.

Europeans are likely to take a just pride in their achievement. But they must guard against Euro-centrism and introspection. If we want to use the alliance as an instrument for keeping the US fully engaged in Europe, and prevent a return to its isolationism, Europeans must beware of becoming equally self-centred. Europe, even pan-Europe, is only the core of a far wider world, and for many others not even that. Merely achieving power is not enough; one needs continually to weigh the justice of its use. That is the rationale which has now led us inescapably to the need to build the European pillar.

Then there are the ever-present out-of-area risks to challenge the alliance's conceptual thinking and actions. Because they touch upon involvements which normally lie outside the scope of the alliance, they may reveal conflicting interests when emergencies ruthlessly place them upon its agenda. As within NATO itself, the remit of regular political review within the alliance needs to be set more widely. That process too should include some crisis management exercises. Preparedness is all—yet it should not be an excuse for retaining large contingency forces, or developing a 'rent-a-threat' psychosis.

Collective security also means taking on the problems of others. That is a new fact with which we may need to come to terms within the EC as well as the alliance and the new pan-European security system. The dangers raised by such problems will need to be pre-empted by political means and, where they develop into a threat, subjected to intensive political treatment. This constitutes a further reason urgently to strengthen the political processes within the alliance.

It is the alliance itself which must ensure its internal cohesion and the continued political commitment of its members. What does not move forward will inevitably roll back. The search must continue for initiatives which will integrate its members more closely. Not all of them need be within the forum of NATO or the alliance itself. The consensus promoted within its councils should, in fact, make itself felt in other fora and institutions. But there is much still to do within the defence and security field. Role specialisation and alternative defence may be some of the available means to display the common purpose and achieve greater integration. Not very much has happened since the classic comment that 'the only thing that the armies in Europe have in common is the air in their tyres'.

Change and diversity do not mean lack of purpose. On the contrary, they demand it, if the strength they can bestow is to be harnessed and channelled to constructive purposes. Similarly, security does not bring political cohesion but is the result of it. And to reach the cohesion we must guard and continually refine our common objectives. That is where the real strength of the alliance must reside. That commonality of purpose is our real store for an uncertain future, the real arsenal which it is the task of the alliance to guard.

The final word

The European-Atlantic agenda as here outlined leaves us with a great many questions. In the final analysis, they all amount to how we can summon the will to address the new tasks. How can Europeans of East and West find the will to trust each other, and on that trust build permanent institutions to keep the new peace? How can the still proud countries of western Europe find the will to swallow the old pride and see a new one born in the prosperity of their Community? How can the peoples of the Soviet republics, in the zest of throwing off their shackles, find the will to seek a new unity among themselves, capable of forming one of the essential building blocks of a vast new security zone? And how can the USA, standing before new sacrifices to right their own economy, find the will to continue to put the world to rights?

In the last resort, the answers to these questions will depend on the ordinary citizen, in Europe as in the US and the USSR. It is he who must feel himself a natural European before the Community can become fully integrated and a security dimension find support. It is he who, newly liberated from long decades of tyranny, must vote instinctively to subordinate that liberty in a greater whole, so as to win a greater security. It is he who must feel the need for the Atlantic bridge to be kept in good order and repair.

Nor is that all. For he is now also required to develop a consciousness of a global responsibility towards the southern hemisphere and
its peoples sliding further into poverty. He is asked to assess the
humanitarian, political and economic dimensions of their condition,
and of the security threats it poses. He is forced to recognise that as a
civic duty as immediate as the destitution, homelessness, drug abuse
and crime in his home town. He is told, indeed, that the whole globe
has shrunk to become his own home, in which he is destroying the
planetary house as much as it threatens shortly to destroy him.

From the nightmare of nuclear holocaust he has woken to a reality
of mad dictators bestriding the desert, brandishing chemical weapons.
He has weathered the chill of the Cold War, only to see it replaced by
the fever of global warming. He has tasted the gift of a world at peace
and without dictators, only to find himself without a job. All that is
good and decent seems somewhere to have a dark side to it. Would he
not be justified if he cried 'Enough!'?

We must believe that our citizen is made of sterner stuff. Otherwise
how could he have survived the forty years of Cold War, the seventy of
Marxist-Leninist-Stalinist terror, or the centuries of feuding through
which we have followed him to arrive here? We must also believe that
his leaders, with all their faults, are still made of the stuff that has
brought us to this moment in history, with our heads held high.
Perhaps their greatest weakness is just that they do tend to listen to
their voters, corporate as well as individual. 'All politics is local
politics,' observed the former Speaker of the US House of Representatives, Tip O'Neill. That means that they do not always lead from the
front, even on the important issues.

Given that the whole future of the now immeasurably enlarged free
world rests on the continued strengthening of the Euro-American
alliance, what should those US politicians be declaring around the
parish pump? What is it that can reconcile their local concerns with
the great issues that are facing the world? What are the words they
should find to bridge the gulf between the concerns of the individual
and the destiny of our civilisation?

'We are a superpower,' they might say. 'No war of any substance
could happen anywhere in the world that didn't affect American
interests. We are a big, visionary and far-sighted country, and
we have to carry the loneliness of responsibility and power. We
have been much criticised for it, but we have the inner confidence and the sense of history to realise the undisputable role of

world leadership for America. We know that our trading patterns, our investment, our people are all over the world, involved in every manner of country. The thing that matters most to America is to preserve stability, prosperity and security, because we could not keep out of any breakdown. So, in our interests, we must stop it going wrong before it can happen to us again.

Now, when we look at the Europeans, can we rely on them? They are all nice guys, and some of us are descended from them––but they are totally unable to do it on their own. And for all the fine phrases and all the new alliances, and all the new jargon—don't put your last buck on it that they won't have to call us in again. The only way we can protect American foreign policy interests is to be there, to stop these things happening again as they have in the past. You and I know that would mean that hundreds of thousands of young Americans will die, because over there they haven't been able to keep their own peace.

'We know we don't have to spend so much money this time because we've seen the Russians off, we've stopped them for the time being. We know we don't need so much equipment over there, and we've got to get our deficit under control. So we're able to bring a lot of the boys back, but we can leave a lot of their equipment there, and hang on to the bridgeheads we have there. But, for God's sake, don't let's go back into that isolationism which has cost this country and her young people so dear in the past.

What we want this time is an insurance policy. None of you would leave your home empty all day without paying a small premium for the certainty that, if it isn't there when you come back, you've got compensation. The best way to think of American foreign policy is as a premium, an insurance premium to make sure that we don't have to send our young people over there to sort it all out again.'[13]

Alas, the world is not perfect; nor is man predictable. We do not know what effect such words will have upon him, or whether politicians will prove brave enough to utter them—especially in Spanish. On the contrary, what we do know is that, in politics, self-interest can be neglected only at one's peril. By the same token, foreign policy is the extension of the national interest. Any politician unable to find the formula to combine that with his more visionary ideals stands to be swept aside.

Politics, moreover, is short-term. Irritation with the chequered responses within the EC and Japan to the needs of the Gulf campaign could inflict long-term damage on the alliance. Worse, hasty tinkering with the military limitations imposed by the post-war constitutions of Germany and Japan could rock the pillars on which the world's peace has rested. Here, too, the politician will need to weigh temporary expediency and short-term goals against the longer-term good.

As with man, so with his works and his institutions. They are like some great orchestra which at times seems driven not by the conductor but by some unseen hand of fury. At other times the score on the rostrum is blank and uncharted, or it shows no key. Most of the time, different sections play in counterpoint rather than unison. There are long discordant passages when one yearns for the harmonies to reassert themselves. One after another, different desks project their voices, some querulously, some plaintively, others inevitably with great clashes of percussion. And then, suddenly, everything is brought together in a great healing resolution.

We have the grace to have arrived at one such majestic passage today. It would be good to think that we might have a hand in completing the score, to engage all the genius of the old and the new world, and for a while to make the harmonies endure.

APPENDIX

West–West Agenda Meeting on the future of NATO London, 20–21 June, 1990

LIST OF PARTICIPANTS

UK

Rt Hon Michael Heseltine MP (former Minister of Defence)

Caroline Anstey (Editor, 'Analysis', BBC Radio)

Baroness Blackstone (Master, Birkbeck College, London)

Nigel Broomfield (Deputy Under Secretary for Defence, Foreign and Commonwealth Office; former Ambassador to the GDR)

Sir Julian Bullard (Fellow of All Souls College, Oxford; Pro-Chancellor Birmingham University; former Ambassador to Bonn)

Lord Donoghue (London & Bishopsgate International Investments, former Senior Policy Adviser to Prime Minister James Callaghan)

Prof Lawrence Freedman (Professor of War Studies, King's College, London)

John Leech (Federal Trust, formerly Commonwealth Development Corporation, Director of Europe House)

Martin O'Neill MP (Labour Party Chief Spokesman on Defence)

Sir Frank Roberts (Vice-President of various Atlantic organisations, former Ambassador to NATO, Moscow, Bonn)

Malcolm Rutherford (Assistant Editor, *The Financial Times*)

David Suratgar (Group Director, Morgan Grenfell & Co Ltd)

Rt Hon William Waldegrave MP (Minister of State, Foreign and Commonwealth Office)

Sir David Wills (Philanthropist, former Chairman of Ditchley Foundation)

Sir Patrick Wright (Permanent Under Secretary of State, Foreign and
Commonwealth Office)

FRANCE
Min Edouard Balladur (Deputy, former Minister of Finance)
Amb Vicomte Luc de La Barre de Nanteuil (Ambassador in London)
Nicola Bazire (Adviser to Minister Balladur)
Adm René M. Bloch (former Director General, International Affairs,
Ministry of Defence, Commander of French Atlantic Missile
Centre)
Jean-Marie Guéhenno (Head of Planning Centre, Foreign Ministry)
François Barry Martin-Delongchamps (First Counsellor)

FEDERAL REPUBLIC OF GERMANY
Dr Klaus Citron (Head of Planning Staff, Foreign Ministry)
Amb Baron Hermann von Richthofen (Ambassador in London)
Prof Dr Michael Stürmer (Director, Stiftung Wissenschaft und Politik
(SWP))
Dr Angelika Volle (Senior Research Fellow, Deutsche Gesellschaft für
Auswärtige Politik)

GERMAN DEMOCRATIC REPUBLIC
Wolfgang Schwegler-Rohmeis (Member of Advisory Board of the
Minister for Foreign Affairs)

ITALY
Senator Prof Beniamino Andreatta (Chairman, Senate Budget
Committee; former Minister of the Treasury)
Amb Boris Biancheri (Ambassador in London)
Dr Ugo Stille (Publisher, Corriere della Sera)

USA
Hon Frank C Carlucci (Chairman, American Academy of Diplomacy,
former Secretary of Defense)
Hon Henry E Catto (Ambassador in London)
Hon H Eugene Douglas (former Ambassador for Refugee Affairs)
Hon Arthur A Hartman (former Ambassador to Paris and Moscow)
Hon Philip M Kaiser (former Ambassador to Vienna and Budapest)
Paul A Laudicina (Vice President, SRI International)
Dr Ivo John Lederer (Senior Director, SRI International, former
Professor of History, Yale and Stanford)

André W. Newburg (Cleary, Gottlieb, Stern & Hamilton)

Hon David Popper (President, American Academy of Diplomacy, former Ambassador to Chile, Assistant Secretary of State)

Hon Ed Streator (former Ambassador to OECD, Dy Permanent Rep to NATO)

Hon John W Tuthill (former Ambassador to OECD, Brazil, Minister to NATO, Director Office of European Regional Affairs)

Prof Harry Woolf (former Director, Institute for Advanced Study, Princeton)

WESTERN EUROPEAN UNION

Amb Horst Holthoff (Deputy Secretary-General)

Notes

1 H A L Fisher, *A History of Europe*, Arnold, London (1942)

2 R Aron, *Peace and War*, Doubleday, New York (1966)

3 M Gorbachev, *Perestroika*, Collins, London (1987)

4 Ibid.

5 D Hume, *On the Balance of Power*

6 K von Clausewitz, *On War*, Book II, Barnes and Noble, London (1956)

7 M Palmer, *An All-European Security System*, European Parliament, Luxembourg (1990)

8 H-G Pöttering, *Die Architektur einer Neuen europäischen Friedensordnung*, Neue Zürcher Zeitung, 11 April 1990

9 C Layton, *A Step Beyond Fear*, Federal Trust for Education and Research, London (1989)

10 F A M Alting von Geusau, *The Spirit of 1989*, Wyndham Place Trust, London (1990)

11 *The Times* 16 July 1990

12 E J Streator, *Arms Control and the Third World*, Brassey's, London (1988)

13 Wording proposed by Rt Hon Michael Heseltine MP in replying to a questioner

Index